One Moar Paradigm

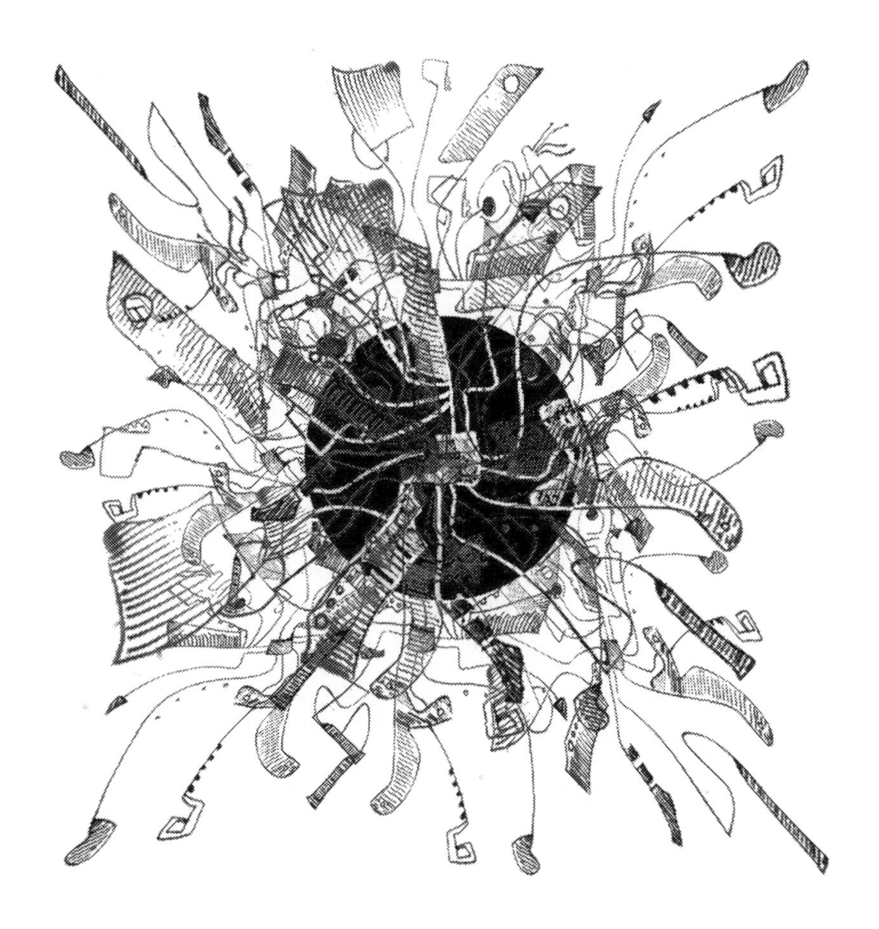

Ian Moar

Balboa Press books may be ordered through booksellers or by contacting:

Balboa Press
A Division of Hay House
1663 Liberty Drive
Bloomington, IN 47403
www.balboapress.com
1-(877) 407-4847

Because of the dynamic nature of the Internet, any web addresses or links contained in this book may have changed since publication and may no longer be valid. The views expressed in this work are solely those of the author and do not necessarily reflect the views of the publisher, and the publisher hereby disclaims any responsibility for them.

ISBN: 978-1-4525-4511-0 (sc)
ISBN: 978-1-4525-4513-4 (hc)
ISBN: 978-1-4525-4512-7 (e)

Library of Congress Control Number: 2012900151

The author of this book does not dispense medical advice or prescribe the use of any technique as a form of treatment for physical, emotional, or medical problems without the advice of a physician, either directly or indirectly. The intent of the author is only to offer information of a general nature to help you in your quest for emotional and spiritual well-being. In the event you use any of the information in this book for yourself, which is your constitutional right, the author and the publisher assume no responsibility for your actions.

Printed in the United States of America

Balboa Press rev. date: 3/19/2012

One Moar Paradigm

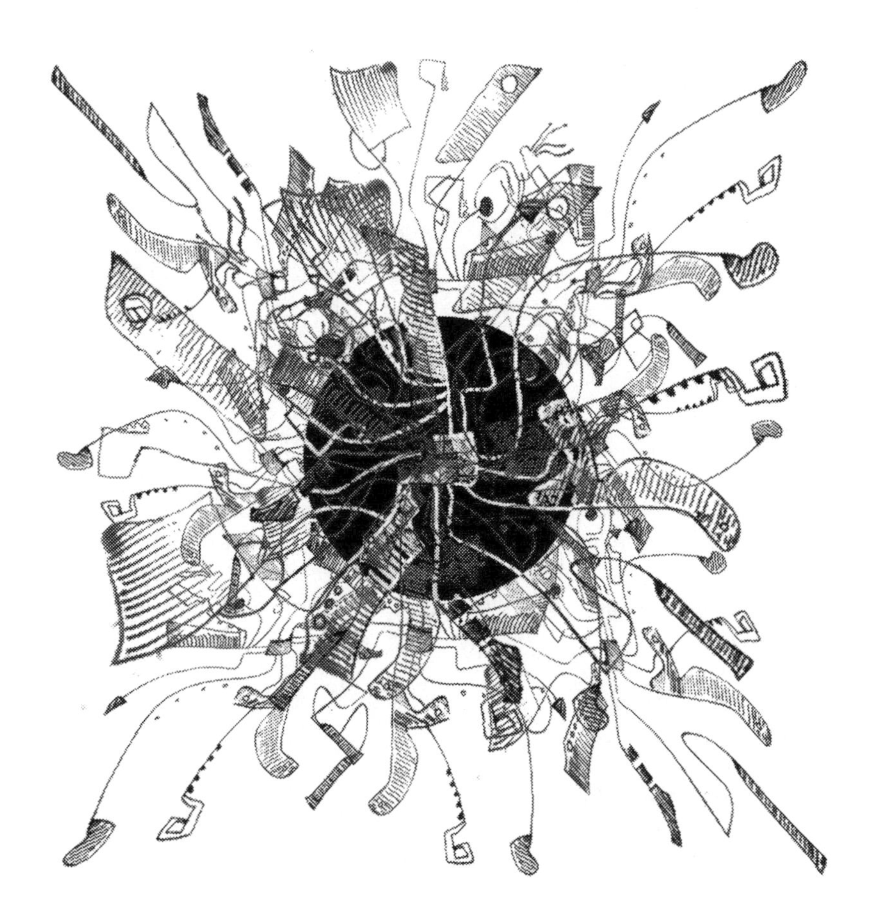

Ian Moar

Balboa Press books may be ordered through booksellers or by contacting:

Balboa Press
A Division of Hay House
1663 Liberty Drive
Bloomington, IN 47403
www.balboapress.com
1-(877) 407-4847

ISBN: 978-1-4525-4511-0 (sc)
ISBN: 978-1-4525-4513-4 (hc)
ISBN: 978-1-4525-4512-7 (e)

Library of Congress Control Number: 2012900151

Printed in the United States of America

Balboa Press rev. date: 3/19/2012

DEDICATION PAGE

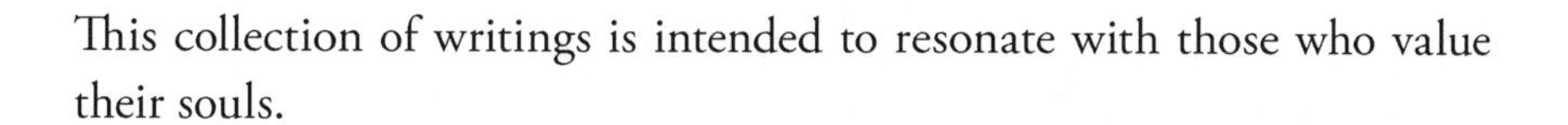

This collection of writings is intended to resonate with those who value their souls.

Friend and world-travelling artist Russell Maier has kindly consented to my use of his artwork titled 'E-scape . . . from Complexity' for my cover art. It would honour both myself and Russell if you would visit his personal website as well as the on-going blog he has created that monitors his challenging travels. Thank you.

www.russs.net

EPIGRAPH

So, there is nothing more difficult to undertake, more perilous to conduct, or more uncertain in its success than to take the lead in introducing a new order of things.

- Machiavelli

It takes only one independent and effective rational mind to change the paradigms of understanding for the rest of mankind.

THE CLOSING OF THE WESTERN MIND
- By Charles Freeman

I knew, further, that only a new paradigm, some genius bursting full-force on the social scene, with lightning in his hands – could break the sodden mass of our heavily sedated, comfortably polluted, self-destruction.

THE BOND OF POWER
- By Joseph Chilton Pearce

AUTHOR'S INTRODUCTION;

Quite frankly, I don't know why I bother, because ultimately, it seems, my attempts to make contact with your soul will prove a fruitless endeavor. In a sweeping generalization, I'd say 95% of the human population has neither use nor respect for the human soul - maybe even 99%. Even though I have always yearned to have it happen, I have yet to decently connect with another soul at a deep level and then see where that potentially very powerful connection will take us. I wonder if I ever will?

Is it simply a question of having a different type of consciousness, perhaps, than anyone I have ever encountered? Is it that I'm trying to latch onto some part of another human being that simply doesn't exist?

If I was of a different temperament, I ought to have become rather depressed over time, but instead seemed always hopeful that some powerful and unique contact or connection with another at a soul level could be made. I am still waiting expectantly for that to happen.

The book you are reading is a record of perhaps my most intense and long-term attempt to connect with another human being at a soul level. It was also my first written attempt at sharing my discoveries of a metaphysical understanding of life with someone else. In fact, it was my relationship with this young man itself that encouraged me to formulate this insight of mine in a substantial way.

In the mid-nineties my parents moved from Ontario, Canada, to a small town called Cochrane, 20 minutes to the west of Calgary, Alberta. They had bought a shell of a condo in a new development and my youngest brother and I choose to design the interior layout and build as much of it as we could, using just enough of the developer's sub-trades to ensure the home warranty remained valid.

We bought the materials we required at a large building-supply outlet on the western outskirts of Calgary at the time, and I met and got to know a young man named Jason at the service desk, who often wrote up our orders.

Jason and I met for an occasional Denny's breakfast on some Sunday mornings, probably half a dozen over a year's time. Jason was studying for an undergraduate degree in Psychology at the local University of Calgary at the time, working at the lumber dealer each summer to help defray his university expenses.

We also exchanged this whole series of letters, and I believe they can stand on their own, as they seldom refer to things we talked about during our long 3 hour breakfasts together. If you've done any of your own soul work, you'll maybe easily slip into its rhythm, sometimes taking on Jason's or my positions as the story unfolds. And undoubtedly your own.

I was the first gay man Jason had ever encountered and that issue occasionally reared its theoretical 'ugly' head in our discussions. If it's an item you yourself are abnormally uncomfortable with, then I suggest this book might not be for you. Perhaps you should close the book right here, although the issue and the way it's presented is in no way shocking. You also ought NOT to read the one item titled 'Why Christians always go crazy about queers' that appears in the appendix.

I do not consider myself an enlightened being, nor do I strive to be one. Nor am I an intellectual, which you'll perhaps quickly ascertain as you read this book. I'm confident, however, that you might find my approach both penetrating and compassionate. I believe I've always been rather easy to get along with, perhaps just a so-called typical Canadian. So be it.

My metaphysical understanding of life is presented about two thirds of the way through this correspondence with Jason, and you perhaps need to know at this point that our entire relationship changed direction after that presentation was made. It had nothing to do with my theories, however - so I will add a portion, perhaps an extension of this introduction, into this book at that point to present the circumstance that ultimately changed the nature and direction of the relationship between Jason and me.

I should tell you that these letters between Jason and me basically appear the way they were presented. I have done some minor editing for grammar but other than that the conversation between us remains intact.

June 16th, 1996

Ian Moar
***Christleton Ave.
KELOWNA, B.C.
861-****

**** EagleBay Road
SHUSWAP LAKE, B.C.
675-****

****Riverview Circle
COCHRANE, Alta.
932-****

Jason;

There you go - all the places you can find me, all the places you can go whenever you turn in my direction.

Saturday morning in Kelowna - somewhat overcast, so I'm not drawn to the outdoors, allowing me to complete this more important work, getting a message to you.

I've been spoiled with a word processor, it being up at the lake and not operating right now - so this electric typewriter will have to do. But with it I know this note will be much shorter than it would otherwise, which may, in the end, be a good thing.

I told you on the telephone, Jason - of my difficulty in remembering how 'real' you were - that our breakfast together had really happened. Perhaps you can imagine how even further away from that I am now, sitting at a dining table on the other side of the Rockies from you.

So why am I writing? What am I doing?

Jason, I think every free time slot where I've had time to think since I had breakfast with you, has been filled with ideas and imaginings and thoughts about you, about situations, about possibilities. And those are exactly the types of thoughts that enhance my life. They're important and significant.

But I told you on the phone that a couple of things came to mind after meeting you and I'd send them by mail. They'll constitute the bulk of this package - so I'd better outline why I think they're here.

I could be wrong here, young man, but I believe you and I think quite a bit alike. You understand and complete thoughts or ideas I have just like I do, although I think you do it faster. Therefore, I have a hunch that you'll like reading some of my pieces - that you'll get into their 'flow' quickly and smoothly.

I think it important for a number of reasons (which we can talk about sometime) that we both get ideas down on paper. Our stuff takes time to play with, to understand, to integrate, to develop. My two attached writings to you will be an example.

And an ongoing struggle I have, which you may well have inherited too, is a serious difficulty in finding someone to really talk to – I'm hoping I've found someone like that in you, and reading these pieces will perhaps confirm or destroy that imagining.

Jason - I think you and I may have some significant connections. Those are things I'd like to talk about next time we meet, so polish up any of your feelings of destiny or purpose in life, or get ready for me to polish some for you.

But for that you need pictures, a vision of life, a developed world-view. And I think that's why these two pieces go your way. The first one is an 'overview' of 'the' situation, the second an 'overview' of 'my' situation. But they're only overviews, statements or slices taken at one point in time in regards to the 'stews' I find myself in.

I think I've written a lot of stuff over the years, Jason, and I think you'd enjoy reading most of it. Just as I'd like to read most of what you have to tell us. I'm not wondering too much why only these two pieces came immediately to mind after meeting you – I'm just trusting they're enough to fill the bill – whatever that bill is.

And so the first one deals with a type of understanding of our general position of humanity at this point in time. The second deals with my general position in relation to the overall position. What will be, I suspect, the most intriguing question – is what your position is and will be? What is and will be the story of your life?

The first piece is two-part - one being an article on morality published in the Vancouver Sun a couple of years ago. The second part is my response, submitted, but to the best of my knowledge, not printed. Try to read the morality column completely, as it presents a world-view and probably reminds you of the arguments you've had with your Christian friend. My piece is then but a counter position, a completely different point of view. But I'm getting redundant.

Maybe you should also try applying this test to both sections. Which piece is 'static', dead and unmoving? Which piece is 'dynamic', encouraging change, growth, understanding, responsibility, participation? Which of the two would you prefer to live under. What system or understanding will you develop that'll supersede both of these? And what system would make you really care?

And the second major piece is just a letter to an old friend, but in it you'll find a couple of ideas we've already mentioned, as well as my take on my position at the time. My take on my position now, Jason, mysteriously includes you, and so I know I'll be devoting significant energy into understanding, appreciating and developing the relationship you and I have founded.

But just as I am half of the mix, you are the other. I think that our breakfast together, the inclusion of these particular writings as well as accompanying thoughts and feelings from both you and I, will somehow influence or maybe even direct our future pathways. What I'd like to know is how you're handling all this to this point. Do you like it? Fear it? Both?

I want to find out. I want to push our possibilities. So when I get back to Cochrane, probably early in the week of June 24th, I'll give you a call. I think we need a bike ride in the country and a meal together. I think we need to create a space, a time, for whatever potential we have in each other's life.

So, I'll talk to you soon. And keep those ***** customers smiling!

Ian

July 13, 1996

Ian Moar
**** Riverview Circle
COCHRANE

Jason;

I don't know if I should be doing this or not. I'm sort of feeling like I did earlier this week when I ran out of gas in one of my brother's trucks. The second tank was completely full (the gas gauge told me that) but mechanically it wouldn't switch from the empty over to the full tank. So I walked a mile for gas, put it in the empty tank and will use that tank only until the problem is found. What was frustrating was in knowing one tank was completely full but I couldn't get at it or use it.

And I find myself about completely out of gas too. My work in Alberta has dragged on from the intended one month to three, with at least another to go. My second tank of gas, the one I access when I communicate with you, is full (my inner gauge tells me that) but I don't know if I can access it. But I'll try.

And I think what I'll try to do in this particular piece is perhaps just round out or add to some things that we've already handled somewhat. I know that whenever you and I talk about something or bury ourselves in some matter, afterwards other pertinent thoughts always arise and sometimes need to be included. That we should always allow time to include continuing thoughts from previous things we've touched on.

I have absolutely no idea or sense of whether or not you'll ever make contact with me again, Jason. What I do know is that it would take a degree of effort on your part and I can't 'read' your willingness to extend that effort.

Should we continue to relate, it will take care of itself and would need no comment from me now. However, if there is no future of any kind for us, then I think I do want to make some comments.

So what I think I would like to do, Jason, is just tell you about some things I've learned (and need to remember) from our encounters and perhaps also a couple of things I see when looking at you. So let me start:

(A) When we last met, you quizzed me like an old grizzly bear about motivations I might have in relating to you. Now I don't know about you, but I don't go into any situation knowing everything about it beforehand, so good questions from you inspire me to try to find the answers too. I think I expressed some motivations to you then, and would like to add to that now.

I feel that the over-riding reason that I'm in your life, Jason, is simply to encourage you to become everything you can be. I admire your stubbornness and resistance to being pushed in any but your own direction, in your fear of me trying to convert you to 'my' religion. I just hope you have as vigorously questioned the influence and directions your family, your friends, your education, and your culture are pressuring you into taking.

I sense I am one of the few (and perhaps only) person you'll ever meet whose 'reality' is close to your own. If that were true, it would be wiser for us to encourage each other, rather than antagonizing or frightening each other off.

I think I'm in your life, Jason, to kick you further up the road in regards to understanding differences in people, in discrimination. I'm probably not overjoyed in being the first gay person you know, but I am glad you were smart enough to know that it's something you'll need to learn how to handle. That how you react to me, in this as well as in all other matters, tells us far more about you than it does about me or the issue at hand. That, as you noted, you couldn't very well hang a shingle on your practice door saying 'No Gays Allowed' - for that would heavily indicate that you yourself needed the same types of counseling you hopefully were giving your clients.

And perhaps above and beyond everything else, I think I'm here to be your friend. That when the long days are over, whether they were days of battle or of joy or of just simply living, that I think you'll recognize that. And appreciate it.

(B) I sure as hell hope I can learn this lesson, Jason, and perhaps sharing it with you, on paper, will help to reinforce it.

I guess I'm not sure whether being told ten years ago about finding a 'partner' concerning my project was helpful or not. As I mentioned to you when I discussed it, I had more or less dropped the idea two years ago after being seriously rebuffed, but it cropped up again when I met you.

Nobody knows what I'm taking about in the context of the lives we live. I guess I've hoped to find someone who can speak the language of another reality while existing in this one, and I should learn that it's just not so.

When and if the situation changes, then those who know how to speak the language will come to the fore. Perhaps only then will I make sense to someone else.

I wish I could get off my ass and muster the tremendous amount of energy required to challenge and change the system, the one most regard as 'reality'. I guess the idea of having someone to do it with made it sound easier and perhaps not so crazy.

Jason, I want to encourage or instigate the types of changes we need to allow people to become what we've been created to become. And I think that's your calling too, and your choosing psychology is the closest thing our culture offers that echoes that yearning. Years ago you probably would have become a Catholic priest, because it also was the accepted and established social avenue designated for such individuals for the milieu that then existed.

We're in a time frame now where new dynamic ideas are needed and you're going to find some of them, Jason. The priesthood looked after the religious eras, psychiatry the scientific, and you and what you discover perhaps the next.

Which reminds me of a recently read quote, from 'PHYSICS FOR THE REST OF US,' by Roger S. Jones;
"Every culture in history has invented or 'received' a creation myth whose express purpose was to rationalize human existence, to tell us who we are, how we got here, and what our value and purpose are. Indeed, it is the job of creation myths to tell us the meaning of life. Modern science does precisely the opposite. For the first time in history, a culture has conjured up a story about itself that altogether denies any meaning, value or purpose in human existence. This is far more perverse than simply fouling our own nest: this is a total denial of any need for a home, a haven, or any sense of belonging. In place of a nurturing, participatory universe, we are supposed to sooth and pacify ourselves

with a detachment and objectivity toward our environment which can only be considered pathological."

And perhaps one of the toughest lessons you'll have to learn, Jason, is whether you can belong to and support the system we find ourselves in. Perhaps a present difference between us is that I'm on the outside looking in at it and at you, while you're on the inside looking out at me, perhaps pitying me, perhaps just wanting me to wander off. And me perhaps presuming that you belong out here, with me.

Another quote, from 'BEGINNING AGAIN,' by David Ehrenfeld. (The thought just crossed my mind, Jason, that probably someday I'll be quoting you);

"The business of prophecy is not foretelling the future: rather it is 'describing the present' with exceptional truthfulness and accuracy.

False assumption and pretense are the enemies of prophecy, and our society is increasingly built on these destructive elements. The tragic discovery made by King Lear was that in a corrupted society, vision and understanding can only come to those who are somehow distanced from the corruption – distanced by wilderness, distanced by blindness, distanced by madness. Lear would not have found his vision today. The twentieth century co-opts its visionaries."

(C) A couple of things come immediately to mind when I look at you, Jason. I'm becoming quite redundant in saying this, but I always marvel at how you seem to manage things so well, and so quickly. I'd be that proverbial rich man if given a dollar for every time I've been rejected when sharing my homosexuality with others. You seemed to recover from falling over that precipice by realizing that you might be better off in the long run not to go too bananas over that issue with me.

A touch of sadness creeps in when I envision how you too might share the experience of rejection by others as you go your way. May you too once in a while encounter someone fair. This sad feeling made me look for an old quote by William Makepeace Thackery, who said:"I never knew whether to pity or congratulate a man on coming to his senses."

Because becoming a conscious, responsible, autonomous being, Jason, will eventually force you to experience personal choice and aloneness that might make you crave for having someone else make the decisions for you, for someone or something else determining what was and what was not possible to do.

When I've been at ***** and had to wait in line for my number to be called, I have watched you work. What jumps out at me is the dedication you seem to give whomever you're dealing with. You seem to concentrate so deeply on the matter at hand that I wonder if you're oblivious to other things going on around you. Some people can do one thing while holding a controlling interest on everything else going on about them, but I don't get that sense from you.

I find how you do this fascinating, and would be led to believe that you handle everything similarly. Maybe that's why you appear to be so fast - that when you're taking care of business, that's exactly what you're doing - taking care of business.

And I think I'll finish off by just commenting on how much I like your 'spirit.' You can ride pretty closely right on top of some line you're following. You seem to have the balls to push convention out of the way. You have a type of daring perhaps I wish I had. So keep it alive.

I don't know if you need to be told this again or not, Jason, but you're important in my life. That no matter what I'm doing, it'll only be what I'm doing at the moment - that you would always have precedence. I would move anything I'm doing out of the way in order to respond to you.

I guess what I'm saying is that I don't want you to ever hesitate if you want to contact me, either by phone or by mail. The only hesitation I would advise is if you considered dropping or severing everything between us. Both of us would lose, and neither of us need that.

It's awkward for me to exit this letter cleanly. Maybe I'll use one last quote to mirror my thoughts of what you're doing, trusting that you'll see what it's saying.

- from 'The Velveteen Rabbit' **"REAL ISN'T HOW YOU ARE MADE YOU BECOME"**

Ian

AUTHOR'S NOTE;

I mentioned two accompanying articles or letters in the previous letter to Jason that have been excluded from this text. They may or may not appear in future books - should there be a demand. Those collections would be titled MOAR ON HIS OWN and MOAR LETTERS AND MONOLOGUES, should they appear.

Ian, July 22, 1996

Initially I would like to apologize for taking so long to respond to your letter. I would have preferred to contact you in person and talk to you face to face but I have been really pressed for time this week. Since it has been several weeks since we last talked, I have been thinking a lot. I realized significantly after reading your letter that you're right; it is my culture and the society I live in that has caused me to be afraid of anyone who is not like myself.

I have to admit that that was my initial reaction when I found out about your "religion". After thinking about it for a while, I decided that just because someone has a different sexual orientation than I do doesn't mean they're still not people. This decision is based on similar criteria that my anti-racism position is. Just because someone is of a different color or speaks a different language doesn't mean they're not people - just like me.

Besides, we all have several things in common, one of which is a soul that shouldn't be deemed any more important than anyone else's. Although I have to admit that when people make racist jokes or comment on homosexuality, I don't always have the strength to stand up for what I believe in. Perhaps now that I know someone who is gay, I will have more courage to stand up for my opinion and let people know that what they are doing is wrong, and it is unjust to criticize people just because they don't know anything about them.

I also feel as though I would learn a lot from you and your experiences. I don't believe I should miss out on this opportunity simply out of fear of the unknown. I would prefer to convert that fear into a desire to learn and understand how and why you are different than myself.

It is not to say that I'm interested in adopting your "religion" but I would definitely like to learn more about it. I feel as though the only thing that could sever the bond between us would be any attempt on your part at trying to change my sexual orientation. Since I don't feel any immediate threat, I feel that I can be comfortable enough around you to continue to be myself.

However, for me, a much larger threat or fear occurs inside me. It is perhaps my greatest fear in life and that is to become part of the mainstream in society. I have spent a great deal of time watching people and I have concluded that I don't want to be like them. There are so many conventions out there that are constantly shoved down our throats and I don't think this is right.

I remember in one of my social classes in high school when we learned about a philosopher names Jean-Jacques Rousseau (I think that was his name). He said that "society corrupts man." Although there was a lot more to it than that, my poor memory is not choosing to be any help to me at this time. Regardless, I really agree with his view.

This is not to say that if there was no society that we would be better off, but the one we're in now is really corrupting us all. I feel that it is the people that ignore or go against the conventions (ie. you) that are real people. I find that you're not a mindless, group following zombie like most of the people I observe and know.

It is not to say that I want to be exactly like you but would like to have the freedom of thought like I believe you do. To me this is perhaps one of the most important things to attain in life and I fear my own corruption very much. Perhaps this freedom of thought is in my own power to attain but I lack some of the willpower necessary to exercise this freedom. This reminds me of a psychologist named Albert Maslow who came up with the idea of the self-actualized person. This whole concept, which I'm sure you've heard of, consists of expressing one's real self. Now this real self is obviously different for everyone but the method of expression is always the same. You simply be yourself and adopt almost a 'I don't give a shit!' attitude - but not to the point where you're an asshole but simply don't allow yourself to be influenced by other people.

This influence can be positive or improving, but don't let people stand in your way of being "you". I think both you and I suffer from this. We tend to seek and bond with people like ourselves, and I especially shy away from people who I feel are not like me. If I had more internal strength I would not need to fear these people because I would have more confidence in myself. I think this might be because I seek to know who I am at 19 years old when I still have so much more discovering to do. Most people I know don't feel this desire or need because everyone is just living, rather than observing like I do. I'm still trying to decide how to live and miss out on a lot of actual living that I could be doing.

When I read about the self-actualized person I decided I wanted to be like that. In a way, I wish never had. I think I may be pushing this idea a little too quickly for myself. Oh well, I guess that's my problem.

Well, I certainly hope to see you before you leave for B.C.. I'll try to call you before you go but if not call me and let me know when you're leaving. I'll be very busy for the next month because I have to find a place to live and get ready for school. So I guess I'll see you soon and we can talk a little more about what life is about.

An aspiring self-actualized person

Jason

August 2nd, 1996

Ian Moar
**** Riverview Circle
COCHRANE 932-****

Jason;

Would you like to know how many hours it took me to get up the nerve to open your letter? Must've been about four, it just sitting there while I ate, worked in the garage, went with a neighbour up 'Gas Plant' Road to watch the sun set, then a deserved shower, into bed and finally your letter.

I was a little nervous, a little afraid, surprised at my sensitivity about the whole issue, wondering if you were about to toss me out of your life or not. And needlessly so, for your words, as usual, made me glad to know you.

Can I start this letter by just relating a few things bouncing around my brain in response to your letter? I should tell you that I spent a couple of hours developing some thoughts for you on paper last night, but it got too involved or too heavy - so I'm starting again.

Jason, when I mentioned my 'religion' in my last letter, I didn't mean my homosexuality at all. I meant my beliefs or value system, but given the revelation you had just recently wormed out of me, it is understandable how you applied one thing to the other. What we should both do is go back to that letter, me reading it with the point of view you had on it, you reading it with the one I intended. And it may well be pivotal, with both sexual and spiritual intonations to it after all.

I'd like you to sometime tell me all you know or understand or think or feel about our 'souls,' Jason. You mentioned that; "we all have several things in common, one of which is a soul that shouldn't be deemed any more important that anybody else's." I've never done much work on 'souls,' yet sense importance there. Have you done some figuring out about souls, and would some of what you believe come from your Catholic upbringing or background?

Two small episodes came to mind when you mentioned souls. About fifteen years ago I was having a telephone conversation with Albert (I've given you a long letter addressed to him) when he started to talk about successful cloning experiments going on in Australia - apparently on the threshold of cloning human beings. (I've never heard of any 'successes' since then) So I asked him a typical Ian-type question, wondering if a soul would be present in each of the clones, and if so, would the souls be exact duplicates or clones too? Well, Albert answered that question with the remark that I really needn't worry about whether clones had souls or not, for in his opinion, most people in the world don't seem to have souls. You can imagine some good questions that his observation would prompt.

Secondly, in a poetic letter to a long-time lady friend and after I had come back from many voyages, I said something like; "I used to think we were bodies and had a soul, but after much experience and many observations, I've come to perhaps think that we are souls and have a body." Does that mean anything to you, Jason?

There may be several, perhaps many keys that will help you unlock your potential and your life's work, Jason, and I'm sensing that the whole field of 'souls' may be one of them. You may well be a 'soul doctor' and so any time you devote to soul-work will be worthwhile. In fact, what you most frequently touch when we relate is my soul, Jason. And I wonder if you knew that, and I wonder if you can develop an understanding of the power there?

Change of direction; Thank you for sharing the 'greatest fear' in your life, of being swallowed by mainstream society. I think you already have the one most successful weapon to guard against that happening, and that is your consciousness. As long as you're aware of something, then probably 90% of the battle is won. How else could you do it other than in just keeping an eye on it, knowing yourself and in developing a trust in your own process?

Jason, I don't like you because you work at a store that sells great lumber, or because you ride a motorcycle or part your hair in the middle or because you're a millionaire or well hung or like the colour purple. I like you because of who you are inside and because of how you handle your reality and because of your potential, and all that tells me that I don't think you'll ever get swallowed up by the giant.

Do you remember telling me at our first breakfast your conversation with a girl and telling her that you more or less had to be crazy to do well in this world and how oddly she handled that? Jason, you're too bright to be that type of crazy. Aldous Huxley, who wrote 'BRAVE NEW WORLD,' said; "The really hopeless victims of mental illness are to be found among those who appear to be most normal. Many of them appear normal because they are so well adjusted to our mode of existence, because their human voice (might he also mean their 'souls,' Jason?) has been silenced so early in their lives, that they do not even struggle or suffer or develop symptoms as the neurotic does. They are normal not in what may be called the absolute sense of the word; they are normal only in relation to a profoundly abnormal society. Their perfect adjustment to that abnormal society is a measure of their mental sickness. These millions of abnormally normal people, living without fuss in a society to which, if they were fully human beings, they ought not to be adjusted, still cherish 'the illusion of individuality,' but in fact they have been to a great extent deindividualized. Their conformity is developing into something like uniformity. But uniformity and freedom are incompatible. Uniformity and mental health are incompatible too . . ."

Abraham Hescel wrote; "Normal consciousness is a state of stupor, in which sensibility to the wholly real and responsiveness to the stimuli of the spirit are reduced. The mystics, (and maybe you're a mystic, Jason?) knowing that man is involved in a hidden history of the cosmos, endeavor to awake from the drowsiness and apathy and to regain the state of wakefulness for their enchanted souls."

Robert Anton Wilson, in 'PROMETHEUS RISING,' said; "The average person is philosophically most 'open' and 'curious' before the adult sex role of parenthood is elected. 'After' reproduction, there is little time for speculation, and there is also little inclination."

"Regarding the role of child-rearing as the production of a sane, balanced, creative human being - this has 'never' been the goal of any society in the real world. The traditional child-rearing methods are quite logical, pragmatic and sound in fulfilling the 'real' purpose of society, which is 'not' to create an ideal person, but to create a semi-robot who mimics the society as closely as possible. Very simply, a totally aware, alert, 'awakened' (unbrainwashed?) person would not fit very well into any of the standard roles society offers; the damaged, robotized products of traditional child-rearing 'do' fit into those slots."

"As the accelerated changes now occurring propel us into the most rapid period of social evolution in all human history, we will then need citizens 'who are not' robots, 'who are' creative; 'who are not' docile, 'who are' innovative; 'who are not' narrow-minded bigots, 'who are' explorers in every sense of the word."

He also said; "Stupidity has murdered and imprisoned more geniuses (and more ordinary people), burned more books, slaughtered more populations, and blocked progress more effectively than any other force in history."

"Intelligence is the capacity to receive, decode and transmit information efficiently. Stupidity is blockage of this process at any point. Bigotry, ideologies etc. block the ability to receive; robotic reality-tunnels block the ability to decode or integrate new signals; censorship blocks transmission."

"In summary, Intelligence Intensification is desirable, because there is not a single problem confronting humanity that is not either caused by or considerably worsened by the prevailing stupidity and insensitivity of the species; badly wired robots bumping into and maiming and killing each other."

And now something from my own experience, which I guess touches both the soul-talk and the monster fear simultaneously. Probably ten years ago, I guess, mom was cleaning out old family photos and sent all her kids ones of themselves. I mounted several in frames and hung them on a small wall, but while working on them, I looked at the kid in those photos and thought of some of his stories, some of the things that affected him and pointed him in the direction I've been walking, I guess, since puberty. And this is what I wrote, although some words aren't coming back too clearly in my memory;

PORTRAIT OF THE MAN AS A YOUNG BOY

looking deep
see the sparkle
in his eye
start to fade
as he grows
and turn
to tears

glimpses of life
perhaps already
starting to tear
the gentle fabric
of his innocence

already
sensitive
to the insensitivity
around him

the slow
unending
crushing of
his soul

what
would life hold
and who
would care

well
years and years
have passed
and I am
still
around

sometimes
quiet
sometimes
thoughtful
sometimes
sensitive

and looking deep
and past
the sparkle
that you might
still
sometimes find
in my eye
can you
find him
can you find
that little boy
still
sitting there
still
all alone

and wondering
what life
would hold
and who
would care

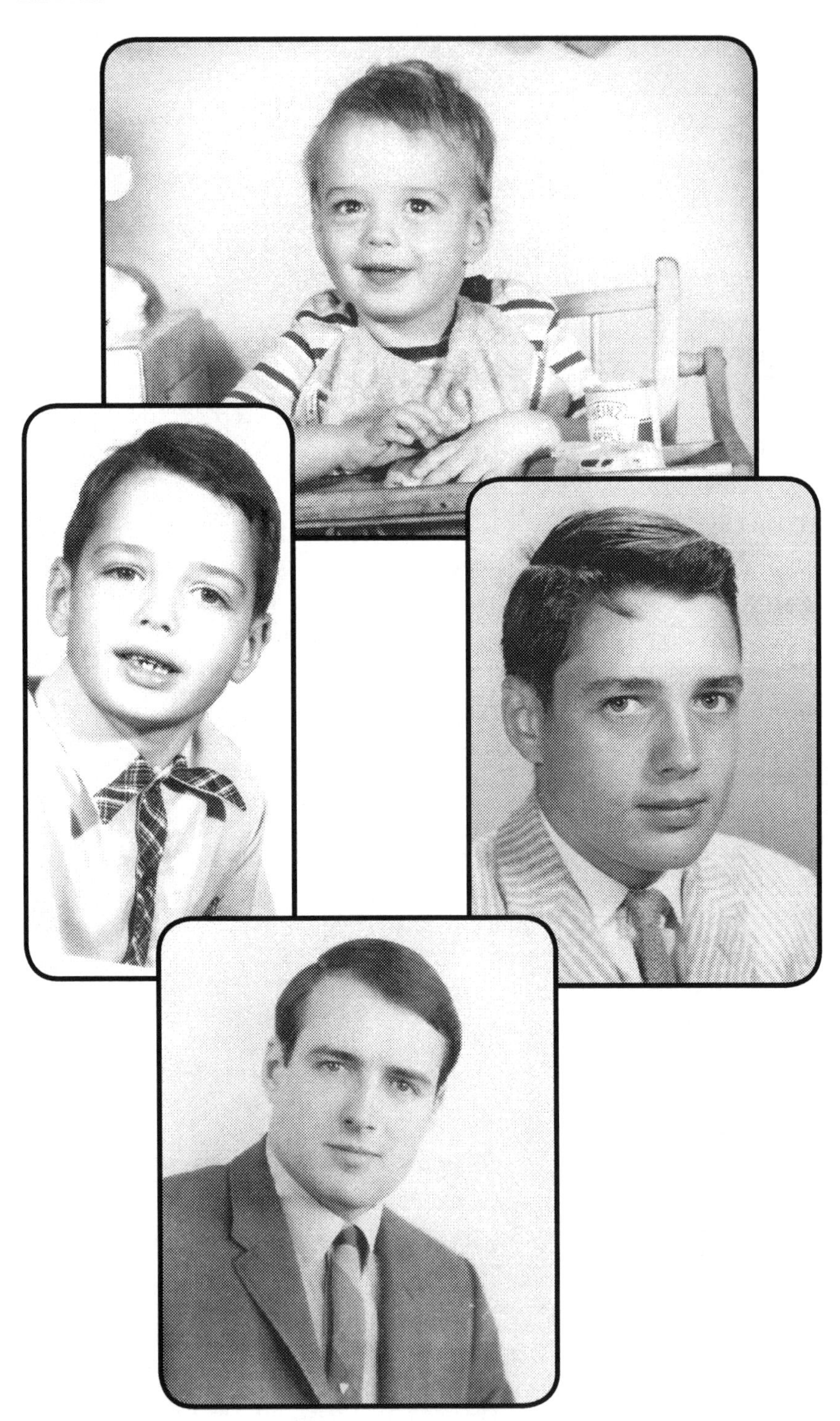

Jason, there are so many things you're going to be handling in life, and so many things that I have to handle - some we get to share, some we get to talk about. I find I want to get into some fairly involved ideas with you, but now sense it time to finish this letter. Twice now I've delved into subjects, spent two to five pages on them, and then backed out. Not them. Not now.

What I would like to discuss in person with you, though, is a couple of things you brought up in your letter. One deals with ' missing out on a lot of actual living that you could be doing,' which may be a price you have to pay for being who you are. Another is the significance of how we affect others, and how we are affected or influenced by them. We need to talk about 'our ideas versus our humanity.' And we can always try to discover more of what the hell we're doing.

Jason, I don't expect to get out of Cochrane for a month or two, so let's each of us let the other know when it's time to get together. And at some future date I'd like your address when you move from your parents' home - I'd rather go to you directly rather than through them.

Anyways, I'm bagged. Long days working, Long hours trying to say something to you. Now I'm just fumbling and mumbling, especially so since another four or five written pages have been axed. And something I need to do before I close, and that is to thank you for not excluding me from your life. It has been so disheartening over the years, to send out so many signs and signals, and have nothing significant come back, that I've needed someone who can adequately respond to my being. I think you do that.

And if I need to apologize for a letter that does nothing but ramble, I'm sorry - but I've got to get it off. I've got to stay in contact with you.

Will probably talk to you soon;

Ian

Monday, September 9th, 1996

Ian Moar
Monday, Sept. 9th
**** Riverview Circle
COCHRANE

Jason;

Sometimes the first sentence is the most difficult to find, and ones I've considered for this letter are;

– Jason, this is my first correspondence to you in your new address - in fact, it may be the first personal letter that you've received in your new abode.
– Jason, I sometimes wonder when it's an appropriate time to write to you, to make contact, and I knew before I had breakfast this morning that now was one of those times.
– I don't know about you, Jason, but I don't like having to do something by obligation, so I can't place others in that position. This is another of my letters to you, just things I want to share, things I want you to listen to and perhaps think about. I'm not expecting you to sit down and respond in writing.

And now that the first sentence has been more than taken care of, let me amble on.

I had a phone call from Vermont this weekend, my first lover from almost thirty years ago keeping in contact. Thirty years ago - God that's hard for me to believe. And someday, not quite yet, I believe he and I will relate at a higher level, he always hoping that we could, me needing to discover and develop that level itself. In fact it's the level you and I relate on, the one you've also been discovering and developing since your intelligence and consciousness were turned on.

And just before waking this morning, quite an extensive dream involving another significant character in my life, where storms and hurricanes and relationships and separations (in the dream) were both commonplace and foreboding.

And as I lay semi-awake after this dream, some insights came my way, and those will be the mainstay of this letter. They are also what told me that it was an appropriate time to write to you, Jason.

A reoccurring question that always surfaces when I think of saying something to you, Jason, is whether I should say anything at all. I respect your desire to learn all the lessons you need to learn at your own speed, in your own way, almost as an isolated traveler on a long and lonely voyage. And I'm glad that question always comes up, because it reinforces the respect, defines our boundaries, makes me pay attention. That's probably another reason I can't expect a response from you, because that would mean I perhaps am looking at you too directly. Better I just take a big round-house swing at you, so you can reflect and deflect. I come to you at an angle great enough where I can both get close enough to acknowledge and love who you are as well as obtuse or abstract enough so that you can glance right off it if you feel you need to.

I have also sometimes wondered how I would have handled your situation - how would I have responded to someone like me in my own life, like I am in yours? Would I accept the intrusion into my most valued private space? After digging through whatever motivations existed (as you and I occasionally do), would I have searched for the purpose and best direction for the relationship to go?

And my answer to those questions would branch off in two directions. One direction would be an unqualified 'yes', because I could certainly have used someone in my life who both understood me and who wanted to understand me. Most people have just wanted me to understand them. And yes, I would have appreciated the comfort of knowing that someone else had a reality that was striking them the same way mine seemed to be striking me. (This is so real for me, Jason, that just putting together that last sentence has filled my eyes with tears.)

I feel that the last thirty years of my life (since I was exactly your age) could have been compressed into five. I didn't need that much time to learn what I've learned, nor to integrate it. You've always thought you're moving too fast, Jason, learning too much too soon, whereas my complaint is that there's just been too much space, too much time taken to get where I've got. This is where I think having someone close by could have encouraged, supported and pushed me to find that place that I had to get to - but faster.

And I'm saddened that amongst the thousands and thousands of people I've met in my life, and amongst the nearly six billion people out there breathing the same air I do, that I never encountered someone to fill that bill. Where were they putting all their attention and their care? What did they see as the human condition or situation, and by what compass, what readings were they using to guide their seemingly rudderless voyage?

And the other direction this inquiry goes displays my own discoveries and understandings of humanity - that somehow history has been unrolled in such a way that the end of the roll, or at least the present roll, can now be seen. The carpet is down, it's flat and it can be seen in its entirety, with its colourful blend of natural beauty and physical tragedy, of its lack of love and overabundance of hatred, of all the things everyone wants to weave into its structure.

And when I look at it that way, Jason, I know I have to be fifty years old at this juncture of time, and that makes it alright. And I also know you have to be twenty right now, that you have to be going at the increased speed you are and able to cope - and that makes it somehow alright for you too.

And so I couldn't have used someone like me in my own life when I look at it that way. But I think your situation is slightly different. I think that if I was twenty today, and in the situation as we find it, I could use someone like me in my life. And so I don't mind being in yours. I don't mind writing when I want, or calling you or saying what I want or feel I need to. And I think you handle it in a very mature way, something I also know I couldn't have done when I was your age.

Anyways, I wanted to talk about an insight on waking this morning, and it's time I got to it. In this dream I had I realized that my purpose isn't in the relationships I have with people, even though I know how important those relationships are to me. So I had to ask - what is my importance in relationship to? It became clear that it wasn't in relationship to the particular events in mine or the lives of others, although they've been significant and important. I had thought that maybe my relationship with the 'process' of life would be where I'd find my importance, but now that rang hollow also. What became clear, (although not crystal clear) was that my most significant importance becomes realized in my relationship with the situation at hand.

That my life-full of relationships, those involving others, those involving the history of occurrences and events, those involving the process of understanding 'processes' - all these folded together to teach and enable me to adequately and appropriately respond to the specific situation at hand, the one directly related to the full unrolling of this particular carpet of history.

And having this insight, presented in the way it was, was comforting. It showed that everywhere I'd gone needed going to, and that it was all gone to to get me here.

And the most significant character I've met here, at the place where I've got to, is you, Jason. But the insight also clearly shows me that my importance isn't in the relationship I have with you (although it's important), nor in the relationship I have with the events of your life (although that's important too), nor in my relationship with the process going on between us and the ones going on between each of us and our own situations (although that's important) - but rather in my (and perhaps your) relationship with the situation at hand.

That I'm here to do something, to do something that has to be done. You and I need to go into it at length sometime - but that gets into the value or belief system, into the vision thing I've mentioned before. But that'll come in time, when it's right.

And the reason I've brought up this insight, this better understanding of mine of what exactly I'm supposed to be relating to, is in how it might have an application in your life. And so in saying, as I often should, that I could be completely wrong here, Jason, let me try that insight on you.

One of the first things I remember telling you (and which seemed to surprise you in a way) was that you were someone who had the capacity to care deeply about people and that you also had something significantly important to tell us. Therefore I would assume your struggle would involve a great deal of work trying to understand humanity and then determining exactly what it was we needed to be told, what we needed to be helped with and how to present it to us in exactly the right way for it to benefit us all. And that, Jason, might well take a whole lifetime to accomplish, its goal monumental and absolutely required.

And so I think your voyage has been well started. Your keen sense of observation probably is responsible for getting you thrown off the common road most of us travel. You're probably hoping that by studying psychology (society's understandings of how people win or lose the game, not acknowledging that society itself sets up the game any way it wants - just another closed loop, with no way out as long as the game is played that way) that you'll get an answer or the answers you need to do your work. At some point I think you'll see that where you need to go and where society's understanding will take you are two very different places - fortunately or unfortunately. And another reason I'm in your life is to help you not be too afraid to leave that future junction and branch off on your own. Your true purpose and fulfillment, I believe, will only be reached by eventually heading down the road that has only your name on it. That's where you'll find what you have to tell us. Any other road you take will only instruct you to tell us what we've already been told countless times, to no avail.

That I think my insight somewhat applies to you. That you've got discoveries to make about your relationships with people, discoveries to make about the particular events that shade and colour our lives, important discoveries to make about understanding how the process and processes of life actually function, but that your individual significant contribution to life will lay in your particular relationship with the situation at hand - what you do with what you've got when you get to that particular point in time and place on that road that you alone travel. What will you tell us from there? Who or what will you be? And where will we all go from there?

And I've become a significant character in your life, Jason, just as you have become in mine. In me you have found a level of honesty and integrity and understanding that somehow you need in order to help you make difficult decisions that'll certainly confront you. You have someone who doesn't know exactly where you're going (and doesn't need to) but knows it's vitally important that you get there and supports and encourages your voyage. You're such a neat package of potential, Jason - that the whole world is arrayed before you, with millions of possibilities, rewards, dead-ends, loves and loses - that watching you pick the ones meant just for you, however they may first appear, will only draw me closer to you.

Which takes me full circle in the insights I had first thing this morning. That by my own relationship with my own situation at hand, with my relationship with your situation at hand, I become intimately involved with all the other levels simultaneously - that my relationship with you at a personal level becomes more relevant, that my relationship with the events and history or story of your own particular life echoes with a more important ring, that my relationship with all the processes you go through and understand enhance my own life.

There, out of gas. And what sense have you made out of this letter, Jason? What sense have you made out of me? And perhaps most importantly - what sense have you made out of yourself? Today? This moment? Prickling your consciousness? Tickling that great soul of who you are? Perhaps bringing an inner smile, a knowing that you've got an occasional arm around your shoulder, a pat on the back, letting you know that you're doing just fine and a can full of confidence to encourage you to keep heading the way you're going.

And I've just realized that I've gotten this far without yet using some quotations, which isn't like me, is it Jason? So let me pump in a few to round out this page, this letter.

- from ONE, by Richard Bach; "A person trusts her life to what she believes. Her ideas have to support her, they have to take the weight of her own questions and the weight of a hundred or a thousand or ten thousand critics and cynics and destroyers. Her ideas have to stand the stress of every consequence they bring."

- from IF YOU MEET THE BUDDHA ON THE ROAD, KILL HIM, by Sheldon Kopp: "And remember, too, you can stay at home, safe in the familiar illusion of certainty. Do not set out without realizing that the way is not without danger. Everything good is costly, and the development of the personality is one of the most costly of things. It will cost you your innocence, your illusions, your certainty."

- from REPORT FROM THE HEART, by Consuelo Saah Baehr;
  "How many mental trips does a human being make?"
  "As many as it takes to convince yourself," answered the mystic."

I like all the mental trips you and I take together. I wonder what we're trying to convince ourselves of? Ah, the mystery continues, and so shall we.

Ian

Ian; October 15th

Well first, as in my last written communication with you, I must apologize for taking so long to respond to your letter. Although it doesn't feel like an adequate excuse, it is the only one I have thus far and that is that school has been very chaotic since it began a month and a half ago. Hopefully you will be able to understand to some degree why my response has been delayed as it has been. Although you indicated in your last letter that you didn't expect a response from me, I just had to put my two bits of effort and input into our relationship. Another reason for my hesitation in replying to you was that I have been trying to take some time to formulate some thoughts amidst my hectic life. Needless to say it has been very difficult to think about some of the material that was quite often the focal point of many of our conversations during the summer. It is even harder when I am constantly reading 100 pages a night from any given text book. Oh well. Before I discuss any of my thoughts or ideas I would like to address some of the things you brought up in your last letter.

First of all I would just like to say that the more and more I think about our relationship the more I have come to realize that I do care about you, me, and our future as friends and companions. Although it is still not clear as to what sort of journey you and I have embarked on I know it to be one of significance in both our lives. I feel that I have bonded with you in a most peculiar way and this intellectual bond (I call it this simply out of lack for a better word) is a very inspirational, directional, and most importantly significant aspect of my life now. Perhaps I disclose this information now simply because I feel more comfortable and feel a decreased need to defend myself around you; that is not to say that I don't want to learn things on my own, or that I accept all that you say or do, but more that I respect and appreciate your desire to influence my life. I fear perhaps most of all the potential complications of this whole situation. Since this time in my life is constantly full of changes and transitions I am afraid of how I may handle this and most other situations. Perhaps my indecision is common to most people my own age but as I walk around campus and look at other people I can honestly tell myself "they are not like me, they are simply by-products of our brainwashed society." I am sure you are beginning to see my connection with this and the thought I brought up in my last letter about our mainstream society. This whole idea still terrifies me but at the same time interests me because I want to learn and know why these people are different. I also want to know what makes me different from them such that I have not been influenced in the same way they have. I am not trying to make myself sound terribly unique; I mean I know I dress, act, and talk like most people my own age but I think the most important determiner of who we really are is how we perceive our own reality. I am quite convinced that I don't think like most people I know. This has been quite an obstacle for me to overcome in my life but since I have met you there is more hope that perhaps someone can and will understand me. I know that you and I don't think exactly alike, but you are the first person who has at least expressed a desire to hear me and understand me. The best part is that I want to hear and understand you as well.

In reference to another part of your last letter, you wrote that you felt that you had many gaps or spaces in your life over the past thirty years. You also mentioned that you thought that you could help "push" me faster than you had gone. Although I don't feel pressured by this but I do not know when I'll be ready to benefit from it. I hesitate to say that now is the opportune time because deep down I know that not to be the case. I feel that I have to mature and develop as a person in order to gain as much as I can from whatever you and I can bring to this relationship. I guess what I'm trying to say (in a most unsuccessful way it seems) is that I hope you have a little patience with me because there are so many things going on in my life that I need to find balance, first and foremost. To me this is very important for my overall health and well-being as a person. I feel that without this I would not be able to be myself or have any insight into how I might better discover who I really am. Perhaps in my view I look at life as a careful balance between what you realize and what you don't realize and without either, neither can exist.

Another thing I wanted to reference in your last letter is when you mentioned my little blurb about society and how I've chosen psychology as a way of fitting in and following this path that I will never discover what I have to tell the world. Well, first of all the reason I am in psychology is because it interests me. The things people do and how they react in situations intrigues me more than a lot of things in life. However, second and most important I view psychology as a source of security in my future life. I mean what if I do have something to tell the world and do take a journey down the "Road Less Travelled", is it worth sacrificing success for it? I don't know, and it is this not knowing that frightens me most. One thing about psychology that does bother me is that it tries too hard to label and categorize people. I hate that about it, because it doesn't allow for people to express any individuality. Psychology now has become a source of deindividuation for us all. It is unfortunate that our society embraces this as a form of medicine or therapy but in reality most of the time it is the label that one is assigned that intensifies any psychological disturbance. Who's to say psychotics are insane? Who's to say I have to look at this person in a certain way so that I can 'diagnose' them? To me it is all so frustrating.

Well, all in all this is the conclusion to my letter. Although I am sure that it is not as thought provoking as yours are but I try my best (especially considering my lack of time). I hope you and I can get together some time soon for a real discussion about life and unravel more layers of our relationship. Until next time,

Jason

Tuesday, Oct. 22nd/96

Jason;

I'm still in the process of recovering from a somewhat mysterious exhaustion deriving from our meeting on Sunday. I've completed some smaller tasks, moved larger ones further down the line until I feel I can handle them properly, but mainly all I've done since then is just rest, tried some contemplating, distracted myself by starting some design work on an adobe-style house I'd like to build someday in the foothills.

And I wondered if you'd been able to switch easily into your studying mode after I dropped you off, Jason - hoping you hadn't been affected to the degree I was from our encounter.

If I had been doing physical labour, it felt as if I'd worked twenty hours a day for a month straight. If I was athletic, it was if I'd run five Boston Marathons in a row with no break in-between. I don't remember ever being as totally exhausted as I was when I arrived home - but now I think I understand a couple of reasons why.

<u>World-shattering Reason Number One;</u> If I'd been driving a car, which I'll use as a metaphor for having a good conversation with another person, all my trips up to this point in time have run into a roadblock soon after we started, no matter where we started from, no matter where we intended to go. In my conversation with you, that car trip hit no roadblocks, Jason - that it only ended when we ran out of gas. We never stopped each other from going where we wanted to go, we never seemed to hit points of disagreement or misunderstanding. We could make trips into who we were, what things meant to us, how we handled things, as well as making some inroads into future possibilities and potentialities. Well, that's a hell of a big map we found ourselves capable of covering, Jason, and I think we travelled a lot of miles and we handled some of it at tremendous speeds.

To further the analogy, I don't think I've ever even had to check my gas gauge before, always having run out of possibilities and understandings long before worrying about running out of gas. You and I give each other so much scope to explore and so much freedom to roam that it feels somewhat like kids in a candy store - an impossibility not to take advantage of. But the price for this new experience, at least for me, was exhaustion. I suppose that's something I'll have to keep a bit of an eye on in the future, perhaps regulating or trying to govern the areas we can effectively handle at one time. Maybe not - maybe it's just something that we can automatically program into our way of handling things.

But let me tell you, Jason, what an experience you and I give each other. Those old neurons in our brains must be firing at an astonishing rate as we probe our understandings of things, as we imagine things not yet realized, as we get to share who we really are and to a great extent the things we might dream about, the things we desire.

And what's also good is that it's no battle - we're not arguing with or making presentations to some God or authority figure, we're not having to justify ourselves or any position we might find ourselves in. All we do is give each other the opportunity to be real, to respect that occurrence, to understand it, to appreciate how rare encounters like that are. And we do it, kid - but it really bags this old man. But I have no regrets and never would - the value of encountering you and allowing the reality of who we really are to shine through is well worth being tired afterwards.

Anyways, I've also structured my life or my lifestyle to give myself the room or the time to recover. Unlike you, I didn't have to immediately turn to other matters that needed to be handled. I guess I'm just hoping that you weren't as heavily affected as I was, and so could make that transition with energy perhaps stored in your youthfulness.

<u>Earth-shattering Reason Number Two;</u> I think, Jason, from the time we left the restaurant we began to handle or deal with possibilities, things we had to do some new figuring on. When we talked about deserved and undeserved consequences, when we touched on you considering a mission God might have sent you on (I need to tell you again - that that was only one particular construct. I asked the question that way because it was the easiest way to probe your present understanding or position in regards to that area of inquiry. There are other ways into that same area that I would prefer to use and that I will use with you in the future. Now, have I got you really confused?) or when you allowed me to speak about heavy influences I've had on others in my life regarding their true sexuality.

I think what happened to me in all of those subjects was that I absorbed or re-encountered the large amounts of energy stored in each of those areas.

It's as if you and I were walking down a hallway, with a multitude of doors along each side that we allowed and encouraged each other to open. But the ones we chose to open on Sunday weren't just closet-sized rooms, where we could get in and out quickly and perhaps unscathed. Instead, I think behind each door that we opened was a hanger-sized space or envelope filled with memories, longings, potentialities, personalities - and with all the energy that surrounds them. For example, when I mentioned my ex-lover who just recently died, somehow, all of the energy of the relationship he and I had, all of the energy of his life and his death experience, all flooded back into my being. It felt like loading all the files of a diskette onto the main memory of my computer - that even if I only want one item, the whole thing floods in. That it's all got to be there for me to be able to find the one thing I need.

And so what I'm saying, and I'm just relating my own experience, not assuming it's yours too, Jason - is that I was overcome by exhaustion not just because of the exciting energy I encounter with you, but that I also stumbled into and somehow picked up the energy contained in every room behind each door that we opened. That's never happened to me before. I've never had to guard myself against that occurring. Boy, Jason, something sure is happening in my relationship with you. It's amazingly powerful and dynamic, different than anything I would have expected - but, hey, that's excellent, and it's all wrapped around you, young man, a mysterious new force in my life.

And having put together those two Earth-shattering reasons has resolved, at least for me, the question of the tremendous exhaustion that I still feel now, two days after the event. It makes sense, and you know how important making sense is to both you and I. So there's my story about that.

I'm just recovering from one of those frights where pushing the wrong computer key combination deletes everything that's been done. There's no way I could have tried to repeat what I've already said in this letter, so into the manual I went and found the procedure for finding data not intentionally stored but unintentionally removed from the operating screens. Whew!

I'm not going to try to handle too much more in this one particular letter, Jason, but I do want to share with you my discoveries regarding those lottery numbers of ours that I tried.

Sometime I'd like to get your take or your opinion on an attitude or a position I've had for years regarding money - I seem locked into a particular position which I can't get out of, and I think maybe listening to your ideas about it might either confirm my position or encourage me to change it. But more about that when I see you in person.

Anyways, I've been trying this lottery thing on and off for ten years now, and wondered if knowing you might be a new and necessary combination in cracking the code, so to speak. Winning or not winning, using your numbers, would also reveal answers to that throwing out of the fleece. Helping me with as yet unresolved partnership possibility questions.

As I mentioned on Sunday, when I tried our numbers the jackpots were notable, starting at the usual two million, then going to five, then ten, finally fifteen. I had pre-purchased enough tickets to cover all of those drawings because I would spend that time up at the Shuswap, far away from any 649 centres.

I knew I had already promised you that if the combination of half your numbers, half mine, won - then I would split any winnings with you. I figured I'd never won on my own, maybe combining with a powerful character like you would make things happen. But honest to God, Jason, as the jackpot climbed I found myself becoming just more and more resentful. I imagined pigging out and winning the whole fifteen million dollars and envisioned having to give half of that to you. Now I don't know how greed and resentment are tied together, but I was pretty sure that a win would probably mean the end of whatever potential friendship you and I were developing. And it wasn't hard to answer the question of which I'd prefer - (a) money without you in my life, (b) no money but you in my life, or (c) some money (meaning mine) and you in my life. Well, I like option number three the most, option two next best, option one the least of all. In fact, I don't consider option one an option at all.

So I breathed a sigh of relief when those particular 649 drawings were over. I was rather disgusted at myself at how easily I became resentful. But I don't think it was greed – I know I need to be financial independent to do the work I must do. Also, there would always be the chance that any winnings might also have to be shared with other Canadians holding similar numbers. No, it wasn't the greed so much as the resentment, but I know the resentment I'd undoubtedly turn your way would really have absolutely nothing to do with you personally. Just my shit about a situation I had created, but you or our friendship would be the main casualty - and I sure didn't like the sound of that.

I also found that I had too easily become preoccupied by the prospect of the money, almost forgetting that we'd also use this to answer other questions, like the one about throwing out the fleece. I still had some residue about the partnership thing, so I used the situation to help resolve that. As you've experienced, Jason, I have relied on the quotations of others as an important ingredient in how I express ideas to others. That all started because I could never find one particular individual in life large enough to be my mentor. Instead, I found and used the parts of others I considered the best, usually expressed in things they've said about what they've thought. Hence, the quotations.

I think I needed to see my partnership question in the same way - that the burden would be too great for any one person, no matter who. Better to break away from that idea, instead letting a number of people fulfill that role, or parts of it. And as I spin in place, looking at those I know, I see that all those mentors whose quotations I use, the handful of characters in my life I value, all of them become a type of partner. And if this doesn't scare you off, Jason, I need to tell you that you've got the lion's share of partnership stock.

I will use you and regard you as being the closet thing I've ever found with partnership characteristics. Yet throwing out that fleece also showed that I better not try to pull you in too close on that issue - better just let you always float out there in your own individuality and freedom, welcoming the times we get to share things, the times we get to feel things, the times be get to be a little more real. And that's a lot, certainly enough for me.

You're the neatest person I know, Jason, even with a majority of the mystery still unexplained. But I think we're heading into the light where things can be more clearly seen, where we realize that issues of doubt, the hesitations and the bewilderments of life have mainly all been left behind in the dark. And I like that.

To give this a wrap, big fella, just two quotations to keep you thinking;

- from THE COURAGE TO CREATE, by Rollo May; " The poet's labour is to struggle with the meaninglessness and silence of the world until he can force it to mean; until he can make the silence answer and the non-being be."

– from your friend, Abraham Maslow; "The very beginning, the intrinsic core, the essence, the universal nucleus of every known high religion has been the private, lonely, personal illumination, revelation, or ecstasy of some acutely sensitive prophet or seer."

What do ya say, talk to you soon.

Ian

Wednesday, Oct 23/96

Jason;

So what am I doing writing more to you just one day after my last letter went your way? Well, Jason, I've discovered another "Earth-shattering Reason or so for the mood or state I've found myself in and wanted to include them with those that went before. The place that I've found myself is a brand new experience for me and I want to explore it and talk about it while I'm in it, rather than waiting for it to pass (assuming it will) and then use more traditional tools like hind-sight to assess the situation. I have a particular feeling about it now which I might not have later, which is not to say that this feeling is truer or more valuable than what might follow but rather that it has its own truth and value attached which I want to respect.

And I think I'm going to have to handle an issue with you, Jason, that I originally thought I could avoid. I'm seeing that I can't consciously sweep it under a carpet, that I have to at least mention or acknowledge it - that it has a particular power or influence on events whether I want it to or not.

I should say a couple of things about this before I get started. Both of us recognize the heavy load you're already carrying, Jason, and I think this particular letter might have a weight to it that's more than you might want to bear. And I don't know how to protect you from that, other than by not mailing this letter or ever mentioning it. But that, to me, would leave it in the same state it's always been, quietly and perhaps seductively having an influence over us anyways. I think what I'm saying here is that in a way I'm sorry about what this letter may hold, that it's something I originally thought I could avoid altogether or at least maneuver around but now see that I've got to put it on the table for both of us to examine.

I also want to help you through this, Jason. I hope that the relationship you and I have already established would allow the following quotation from Scott Peck's THE ROAD LESS TRAVELED to apply to us; "Commitment is inherent in any genuinely loving relationship. Anyone who is truly concerned for the spiritual growth of another knows, consciously or instinctively, that he or she can significantly foster that growth only through a relationship of constancy. One cannot handle issues like dependency and independency, dominance and submission, freedom and fidelity without the security of knowing that the act of struggling over these issues will not destroy the relationship."

Two aspects of that quotation jump out at me, Jason. Firstly, I really hope in our relationship we can talk about anything under the sun without risk that in so doing the relationship itself will break. Secondly, I value the level of honesty and directness we've established - I think I'd be letting both of us down if I wasn't open and forthright with you about this subject - it's too big and too powerful for me to intentionally try to avoid. Or perhaps I should say for both of us to try to avoid.

I should also say that I suspect you might just surprise me as you have continuously done and handle it well - that I could be making more of it than I need to. I hope that's true - but I've still got to give you the space or the freedom to have a negative or perhaps an indifferent response to it. My personal anxiety at this point revolves around the fact that I'm coming at this whole issue from a new direction for me. I'm going to travel down a road I've not exactly traveled before, although some of the landmarks are certainly familiar.

So that's enough preamble, Jason, let me get on with what I want to talk about.

Yesterday I cited two reasons for my present exhaustion. A third one surfaced last night when I realized I'm tired, really tired, of listening to myself. You give me the opportunity to say things others can't handle, Jason, and I seem to have fallen overboard into that freedom. You support and encourage the building of a space where anything and everything can be discussed and in that space I think we'll develop and actually create a reality that both of us prefer. But I guess I see all the words and ideas both behind us and ahead of us and feel their weight. Right now I'm surrounded by a million or a billion words or ideas and I'm tired. I'd sure like to just listen to you for a while without having to engage all the stuff that's sitting inside me.

It's as if a huge dam that has always held back this reservoir full of energy has finally been opened and I've simply found myself awash in the downhill flow. I'm not afraid of drowning, Jason, knowing I'll get a foothold at some point – I'm just experiencing being caught in a flood. And have I caught you out here in the middle of the river with me, Jason, or are you safe and sound along some shore?

And that, finally, sums up my theories about this total exhaustion I've felt this week, Jason, and now I'd like to switch into this other area that the preamble of this letter has hopefully prepared us for.

I've discovered in my life that I receive most insights or understandings I've had about things when I'm lying down. I've felt that the right side of my brain seems to function best when I'm flat on my back - that my mind immediately goes 'logical' or left-brained as soon as I sit or stand up. Now, I've had insights at other times too, but, generally speaking, puzzles get solved in bed.

And when I awoke this morning I wondered if I was still exhausted, if I still felt as wiped out as I did yesterday. The answer was 'yes,' but I also recognized another feeling. I now felt completely hollow or empty, as if my head was like a pumpkin at Halloween, where some large spoon has scraped everything out from the inside walls of my being. I wanted to know what was going on - why was this feeling here?

And what came immediately to mind, Jason, what immediately made sense, was that I was doing something with you that was as hollow and as empty as the feeling inside me. And it came down to a four-letter word called 'love.' I saw that I was having a relationship with you that was different than any I've had with others, and the type of significant difference I now had to look at was that I was 'intentionally' trying 'not' to love you. I was consciously controlling how I felt about you, and that insight prompted everything in this letter.

There certainly seemed to be justification for what I'd been trying to do. I had a history of loving people and having one of two general things happen - they'd either totally reject me immediately or they went through a personal transformation that altered their accepted reality about themselves in some major way. One response was traumatic for me, the other traumatic for them. As I mentioned to you on our walk on Sunday, once I became conscious of how my love for these people affected things, then I started to choose whether I could afford the energy to encourage either of those two consequences to occur. My answer since then has always been 'no' - that I loved these people for things I thought I could find in them but never did - so why should I devote love and energy and time towards something that ultimately held no satisfaction for me?

And so when I met you, Jason, I was already operating in that mode. I'd pretty well given up looking for anyone whose values I admired, someone who I could make sense to, someone worth loving. It was therefore no problem for me to easily respect and honor that directive in your first letter when you said; "I feel as though the only thing that could sever the bond between us would be any attempt on your part to change my sexual orientation." At that point I honestly didn't care whether you were the most macho heterosexual male in the entire universe, the most repressed homosexual on the face of the earth or somewhere, naturally, between those two extreme positions.

Even in that framework, Jason, I think you and I have done really well together. This morning, however, I realized that you are someone I would naturally and in fact eagerly love - and yet I was keeping myself from doing that. You have the types of characteristics I've always looked for in people – and generally I've always loved them and yet I was preventing myself from loving you as I had them. Now that's weird. Here's a dude who deserved to be loved in a big way, but good old Ian was letting his head rule over his heart, afraid because of his past experiences, not wanting to arouse the wrath and fear of this new character in his life.

But the consequence of me trying to consciously control my feelings for you, Jason, has resulted in this desolate and hollow feeling that now pervades my being - and I don't like it. I don't think I deserve it and I also don't think you deserve only my intellect - that when I care for others in a certain way and when I care for the state of humanity in general, should I not treat you with at least the same degree of care?

I mean, I really feel stupid about this, Jason, but I also sympathize with both of our positions. I think you and I need to develop or create an understanding of what exactly is happening between us, because I don't think the word 'gay' adequately covers the space we're in. This same feeling was echoed in your last letter, when you said; "I have bonded with you in a most peculiar way and this intellectual bond (I call it this simply out of a lack of a better word) . . . ."

Jason – when you mention how difficult or impossible it is for you to think the same way as those around you, I know what you mean. But in my life that also extends to the gay community. I think the common qualities I share with other homosexuals are the gifts of creativity, the ability to communicate well with others and the capacity for genuine compassion - all worthy characteristics. And I certainly value being able to share my sexual drive with other human beings - I can't imagine any type of fulfillment without a satisfying sexual component.

But I'm still not comfortable around them, Jason. There's very little about their lifestyle or how they've generally chosen to integrate into the larger community that I admire. This whole sense of estrangement from others makes me remember Richard Bach, in THE BRIDGE ACROSS FOREVER, saying; "I felt like a stranger in a strange land, and decided I'd better not marry the natives."

I sense, though, that this whole 'gay' thing is fucking us around a bit, Jason - that we're so afraid of that potentiality that we're not allowing ourselves to be real and we're restraining ourselves from trying to find a larger or more appropriate explanation or understanding of what's actually going on between us. Am I making any type of sense to you?

I think you and I have a lot of things to do together in the future, Jason, and I want you to know that I'm going to try to turn this around a little. I want to allow myself to love you instead of preventing myself from doing that. I think everything in the situation calls for that - I think we both deserve it. I want to see if we can consciously and actively find an adequate and workable understanding of exactly what it is that's transpiring between us. Both you and I will have an effect on the world, in fact I think a large effect, and I think we'd better be able to responsibly handle the types of energy in the relationship we have before we turn our attention to the outside world.

Now, I don't know how that love will get expressed or how it will manifest itself, Jason - good God, anyone reading our correspondence to each other, any eavesdropper on any of our breakfast conversations would already easily see or hear the love that exists between us. I just want to remove the artificial cap I've tried putting on top of it all, releasing the control mechanisms, allowing instead for both my head 'and' my heart to function at the same time.

I want to easily be able to tell you that I love you, Jason, without worrying about how outside opinions or outside people feel about it all. I want to turn my heart loose so that it can do what it was designed to do. I want to fill that hollow and empty feeling presently inside me with pictures and feelings about you and about what this world has waiting for us to do. I've always known that my heart is one of the best tools I have and I regret thinking that I could relate to you without it.

As you can imagine, I'll spend quite a bit of time wondering how you'll deal with this, Jason. I don't think I've really said anything very frightening - perhaps it's just an apology for trying to relate to you at just an intellectual or metaphysical level, not realizing that, as far as I'm concerned, doing anything important while trying to exclude my heart makes it rather pointless and without much real value.

And I think that's all I've got to say today, Jason. Thanks for hanging on through all this - you and I really are taking care of a lot of business, enabling us, I believe, to be better prepared for what we'll be doing when we turn our energies and attention to the world we find around us.

At this last minute I've decided to include some enclosures. I told you on Sunday that several people I've met on my travels have introduced themselves to me as Jesus Christ Reincarnate, and with that always came their presumption that the entire world was breathtakingly awaiting their appearance, their words of wisdom or salvation. I don't want you to think that whatever you have to tell the world, Jason, will be either easy for you to discover or for the world to accept. You'll have to present some pretty valid arguments for whatever case you're trying to make - you're going to have to be pretty sure of what you're talking about. From my experience, everything's getting really 'tight' and that better understandings sometimes have to be woven between difficult and presently quite comprehensive arguments - there's a lot of pylons that have to be navigated through successfully.

So what I want to do is take one topic, Homosexuality, and give you some personal examples of types of arguments or points of view that are deeply held and have to be understood and appreciated before they can be confronted. I would also like you to understand that my own arguments aren't advocating homosexuality but rather display my attempts to thwart the reams of discrimination that have always been piled up against gay people. I think all these arguments show how demanding it is to grapple successfully with a difficult issue. I think it also represents the types of arguments you'll be facing whenever you present whatever's important to you to the outside world, Jason.

They also display how much energy, attention and passion is required in handling important things in our lives, Jason. In fact, you and I will have to apply similar amounts of energy, attention and passion if we seriously want to try to understand the potentialities that exist between us. We not only have to understand the world, but we have to understand ourselves and each other and how it all folds together. And I think we're both well on the way to doing that, and that makes me really proud. You and I have a lot of valuable things going for us, Jason - and I'm glad that I can be doing it with you.

I have no idea when we'll communicate next, Jason. I suspect we both need some time to have things settle in or settle down - it's a pretty amazing trip you and I are on. So I'll give you a break for awhile - I'll let you handle this however you must, trusting that all this is simply a further development in what transpires between us.

I think I should also tell you that I think it's time I started to try to figure out the best way to present my 'world view' to you. As in most things we've handled, I'll be coming down roads that I haven't traveled the same way with others, so it has to be 'customized' to best fit in with who we both are and how we handle things. I want to present a 'context' (or as I've said before - 'my' context) of the overall situation to you, Jason, since I think it has applications to you and your life. I've also told you that I suspect it might be 'the' context, and since I believe you like how I think about things, then I certainly want to share the 'insights' and 'findings' that I've had in life with you. A big project.

And I don't want to get out of this letter without telling you that I love you.

Ian

Author's note; I attached 6 items to this letter for Jason, all letters submitted to various 'Letters to the Editor' columns in several newspapers in British Columbia and Alberta in the early to mid-nineties. If there is a demand, a book titled MOAR ON HIS OWN will someday feature all my public battles that these 6 items reflect.

However, one particular item will have been mentioned a few times in this book - so I'll include that in the appendix at the end of the book. Its subject matter is 'why Christians always go crazy about queers' and represents the flavor of the items attached to this particular letter to Jason.

I should also mention that the reader can probably now understand or be able to assess the weight I was placing on Jason's shoulders. He really had to plough through a lot of my stuff to stay up with the traffic flow, and we can likely all understand how difficult that must have been for him.

October 29th, 1996

Jason;

In some ways I'm looking forward to the time when we can directly relate to each other both actively and passively. There's so much going on between us now as we get to know each other and as we allow the energy in ourselves and each other to express itself, that it seems foreign to say that I await the time that silence too will become part. That we can be with each other without thoughts or ideas interfering, basking in the sunshine that tranquility can also contribute. But we're not there yet and, speaking for myself, there's no way I can get the locomotive presently charging down its track inside me to simply come to a complete stop. But someday.

I think there's always been a particular motivation behind each piece of correspondence that flows between us, Jason, and in this one going your way I want to outline or share my general understanding about life with you. And even though I'll set it down in a relatively simple and brief manner, do I need to tell you that it's taken quite a bit of time to formulate and to understand and to respect its inevitable consequences and ramifications?

I can state my theories rather simply because there's next to no dogma attached, no developed doctrine or conditioning affecting them at this point. In fact, the great majority of difficulty I've had in creating an understanding that makes sense and is appropriate for me has surrounded my battles in overcoming the dogma and conditioning both inside and outside myself in regards to present belief systems. I should probably remind you, Jason, that I think everyone in the world has a 'religion,' an accepted religious belief or secular understanding of how they think the world works – and so I've also had to plow through the dogma, the doctrines and the conditioning that supports those systems too. There's a lot of bullshit out there and it's pretty amazing how insidious it's been in attaching itself to everything that we are. It doesn't just cling to our bones - it seems able to infiltrate our beings at a cellular level, and with that characteristic and power our drive to reach our true potential has been thwarted.

As an example of this infiltration, Jason, just observe your own personal reaction to my theories. I would suggest any difficulties that arise will come from your own particular conditioning and not from anything in the theories themselves. Concurrently, any agreements you make with them will evolve from discoveries you've made or are making in your own valid and valuable search for meaning and personal fulfillment.

I should start by saying that my general, ongoing, lifelong motivation, Jason, has been to make sense of this whole thing called life. I've been 'into' or studied various systems or beliefs that have made a type of sense for a season - but they invariably became lifeless, static and untrue. I have always gone 'beyond' anything that already exists, searching for an understanding that made sense, held together, had both dynamic and static elements attached, gave life and meaning and contained some love. What I have created fulfills or completes all those requirements - at least for me.

So this, Jason, is the 'context' I've created or formulated that works and makes most sense for me. In its simplicity and development I've discovered that it doesn't seem to get bogged down in dogma, encourages the flow of dynamic energy, retains or upholds personal responsibility and observes true democratic values.

I should also tell you, Jason, that my development of my understanding mysteriously now includes you, so I can't just set you off to the side as an 'objective' observer - that I've drawn you into its context and will invariably make connections with you as our lives unfold.

I believe our universe was created by a loving intelligence whose main motivation was to create a multitude of loving, creative intelligences. The natural or physical world was created and set up to function on its own, under theories of evolution and physical or natural laws.

I don't believe 'God' can be found in nature - only His handiwork can. I don't believe 'God' is some separate 'being' 'out there' or 'beyond' - in fact, I don't think any 'God' exists at all. I believe He 'once' was, but will never show up again as some entity that we can see or relate to.

Mankind, unlike nature, was set up differently in my mind. I think the loving intelligence behind the creation of the universe divested Himself of Himself and instead incorporated Himself into our potentiality. His final step was to dissolve Himself, determining that He would show up in the characters He created, although only in those who developed their 'souls.'

So everything was set up, the physical universe chugging along on its own steam, our human development going through its various needed stages and variations of belief and unbelief. Christians often talk of their 'faith' - but I think any faith humans can muster pales in comparison and significance to the faith the creator of the universe must have in us. Because if we don't find the right way, if we destroy ourselves and the world that surrounds us - then He too will have been totally destroyed. He is nowhere other, nowhere safe and outside. He is nowhere else but in the best place inside you and inside me, Jason - and will not live or exist if we don't.

So He took a pretty big gamble in the way He set things up, but it was the only way He could set things up in order to get what He wanted, to get what was important to Him - humans who could love and who could create as He originally did. He wanted to create many stories, each one human, each one coming from his or her own experience and direction - all heading towards consciousness, towards soul-development, towards perfect love.

And so, when I 'make up' these things or theories about the origins, intentions and potential development of humanity, Jason, or when you try to discover and understand what's of core value to you in your life - then we aren't doing anything other than exactly what the whole situation calls for us to do. Anyone 'not' doing that, anyone 'not' developing their souls or consciousness are in fact being irresponsible - irresponsible to themselves, to you and to me, and to the situation in general.

There are many things, then, Jason, that have to be developed with such a theory. What types of forces are present in our lives that encourage and discourage us from developing as we should? What types of energy or forces are at work in the universe that create and dissolve the tensions required to drive us to reach our potential? What diversions, distractions and immature belief systems enable us to dissociate from what we really ought to be doing? If there is no 'God' as we have been conditioned to believe, then how can we possibly have the confidence and encouragement to believe any 'other' system is the truth? And how could we ever have the nerve to suggest such a system to anyone else, or at least to others who need 'Gods' to believe in?

And what of consequences? Is there really any justice in the universe - will transgressors ever suffer for their misdeeds against humanity? And who would make judgments, and how would they make them? And are we really getting 'there', are we coming any closer to where we ought to be? And what of 'love?'

And how can you and I make things happen, Jason? What types of things would we actually like to see that we don't see now? Can we find available forces willing to work for us?

And could you do what you have to do alone? Could I? Or are there types of agreements that must be made before things work? And how is power developed and utilized, where one value system is brought into competition with an existing value system?

So many questions! So little time left, so few people who really care. So many undeveloped human stories, so many sad and lonely lives. So little love.

And where do we go from here, Jason? What will I see when I next look into your eyes? Fear? Wonderment? Understanding? Love? Who are you, Jason, and what do you mean to me and to my life? And I bet you'll be able to answer that question as deeply as I can - my wonderful and beautiful young man.

Ian

October 31st, 1996

Jason;

If I was to create a brief list of pertinent questions regarding the process of life that I thought needed asking, Jason, it would look something like this. WHAT is happening in the universe and WHY is it happening? HOW did it develop this way and WHERE is it going? WHO am I, WHAT is my connection to it all, and HOW do I develop or realize my potential?

In my last note to you, I thought it best to simply state my own understanding of the general, although specific, origins of life and my perception of the intentions of the creator of the universe. I think I'd like to handle two accompanying areas of discovery or thought, one regarding the FORCES and POWER of the universe and the other, my own particular FUNCTION or MISSION. I sense this letter will only cover the first topic.

I wonder why I'm CAPITALIZING SO MUCH in this letter. Could it be that I seldom use that function on my word processor, perhaps tiring of underlining or using "quotation marks?" Could it be that, just like the TV program W5, those 'W' words always get capitalized when used in that manner - eg; WHO, WHAT, WHEN, WHY and WHERE? But maybe I'm also getting a little preachy, or at least sounding so, and thinking what I'm saying is perhaps more important than it really is - and that I'd better calm down or I'll lose you. I know I don't like to be 'lectured' to, can usually sense when it's happening (like now) and don't want you to have to suffer through it, Jason.

Robert Persig, in ZEN AND THE ART OF MOTORCYCLE MAINTENANCE, inspires the atmosphere that I'd like to emulate in these last few letters to you, Jason - where I outline my understanding of the situation. He says; "The trouble is that essays always have to sound like God talking for eternity, and that isn't the way it ever is. People should see that it's never anything other than just one person talking from one place in time and space and circumstance. It's never been anything else, ever, but you can't get that across in any essay."

FORCES and POWER

I believe that when God created the world and then eliminated himself from the situation, he had to create a 'force' that would encourage his creation to reach its potential. He had already established physical laws or forces that governed the natural world, those being gravity, electromagnetism and the strong and weak nuclear forces. Physicists are hoping to find one universal or general law, or field theory, that can describe 'all' the interactions of the physical universe and to also show that the four forces have in fact evolved from one common 'unified' force or field.

An aspect of this particular research that I find interesting, Jason, is that physicists say that "There is nothing else to be learned from nature other than the limited and statistical information that Quantum theory provides. The theory is 'complete,' and anything it does not tell us may be interesting conjecture or metaphysics, but it is neither observable nor measurable, and therefore irrelevant to science." (from PHYSICS FOR THE REST OF US, by Roger. S. Jones). That tells me that scientists will never be able to find God in either nature or science - all they'll ever find is just more statistics and limitations - never a full or complete explanation for life.

I have never been particularly interested in nature, Jason, and so a 'force' that I would need to understand related instead to us and the position we find ourselves in. What was this other force God created that would directly influence the ability of humans to reach their true potential?

In my own experience I had been involved with what is commonly known as the Holy Spirit - the Christian belief that this 'force' is part of the God-head, one third of the Trinity. It was the 'power' that actually got God's work done on earth. I also witnessed untold accounts of 'success,' where 'positive thinking,' management by objectives, powers of 'persuasiveness' and a multitude of other 'systems' seemed to make things happen.

At the same time I also experienced in a sad and discomforting way the ineffectiveness and failure of any system I myself formulated, valued and attempted to make function. This made me all the more interested in understanding the forces that made things work, since none had ever worked for me.

So several years ago, while spending time with a powerful lady friend who was into a New Age discipline, I wondered if there was a hidden set of 'metaphysical' laws that governed humanity, just as there was a set of 'physical' laws that governed nature. At that point I thought I was going in the right direction, heading into new territory, but I never seemed to get very far - that the laws were either too well hidden or too complicated. So I changed directions, experiencing my own insights regarding this puzzle, and have found simpler understandings of these forces that make most sense to me.

And one struggle I am presently involved in, Jason, and this also involves you and our relationship, is my attempt to now get this force to work for me (or us) so that we can accomplish what we need to accomplish.

I don't know if you remember during our first breakfast at Denny's when I tried explaining 'symmetry' to you? It's the best way I can explain how I think God 'set up' the force that so influences the evolution of humanity, so let me try to explain it again, hopefully more successfully.

If we think of an object, like someone's face, as being symmetrical, then we mean that the left side, say, is exactly the same as, or the mirror image of, the right side. Scientists refer that property in geometry as meaning something is the 'same' at different places - or is a preserved 'shape.' Now when they look at physics instead of geometry in regards to 'symmetry,' their understanding shifts so that some property is the 'same' at different 'times,' where something is a preserved 'quantity' rather than a preserved 'shape.'

What I want you to see here, Jason, is that that is exactly how I think God figured He'd be able to dissolve himself, trusting that His quantity (and quality) would surface again, sometime in the future - this time in number (however many that might be). That the total of all His creative, loving little imaginings (meaning us) would eventually exactly equal the quantity of energy He originally contained in just Himself. That is symmetry in physics, this 'sameness' reflected in time. This is also why I mentioned in my last letter that I don't believe we'll ever see 'God' again - we'll know He's there because we see Him in ourselves and each other. Someday, I believe, we won't see anything other than just the God in each other. Christians would call that Heaven although their descriptions and understandings about it obviously differ widely from mine.

Symmetry tells me 'WHAT's happening and WHERE we're heading. When I want to understand HOW this powerful idea of symmetry works, let me quote <u>PHYSICS FOR THE REST OF US</u> again; "Forces are the result of a breakdown or reduction of symmetry. To restore or correct the broken symmetry requires the action of some external agent or force. A force remedies the broken symmetry. In field theory a force is always tantamount to the restoration of broken symmetry."

Now how do I apply that? Well, at one point in time, God 'was.' At the next point in time, God 'wasn't'- but He or His essence or energy would be restored at some future point. Symmetry would eventually be restored, but symmetry was now broken. And as that quotation stipulates, when symmetry is broken, a force is inadvertently created that strives to restore the symmetry - and only that force can do it.

Now let me slip you into this explanation, Jason. I think that when you (or I) feel driven to find explanations, understandings and fulfillment, it's because we're sensitive to the universal soul 'force' that is trying to restore symmetry. We are being driven to become all that the intentions of the universe want us to become, and only in that becoming can the symmetry be restored. When God is realized in you and in me and in anyone else who's so led, then our own satisfaction and completion will become a reality. To me, it's like going back to the future, that the love and creative energy we find will echo, match or perfectly reflect what originally was and that we're only now on the way to realizing or developing this and its fulfillment will be reached in the future. The force that's driving us was created by the actual breaking of the symmetry, and that force will function and affect things until the type of symmetry that was broken is re-established.

Before I make some comments about characteristics of this 'force,' let me include two more quotations from PHYSICS FOR THE REST OF US; "Even if we don't know exactly how or why symmetry breaks, we do know when it's supposed to have happened. Perfect symmetry and the one unified force presumably prevailed during the first flickering instant after the universe was born." Now remember, Jason, this guy's talking about physics - it is me who is applying this to reach a metaphysical understanding of HOW we got to where we are. To me, the physical forces scientists are studying here are geometrically symmetrical to the metaphysical forces I'm trying to understand.

This second quote is one that'll really make us think; "The world is so symmetrical in 'supersymmetry' theories that there is no distinction between the interacting and messenger particles. The particles that sense the force and the particles that transmit the force are interchangeable. In effect, there is no meaningful difference between the particles and the forces. They are one and the same."

If you and I are the 'particles' that 'sense' this metaphysical force, Jason - then it means we would also be the particles that 'transmit' this force. Simultaneously, this quotation would also suggest there is no meaningful difference between us (the particles) and the force itself. We are 'one and the same.'

This suggestion or possibility tells me, Jason, that not only do we feel the force working on us or in us, or that we'll transmit this force to the world around us, but we may, in effect, be the force itself - that it's all interchangeable. I'm not sure if I want to go in that direction with my understandings, but I'll certainly put it on a mental shelf for further consideration.

At this point in time, though, I'd like to list a few characteristics of the force I think exists that makes things work. I may throw this whole lot in the wastebasket at some point, but let me try them on for size.

1. Christians believe this force, or Holy Spirit, is a 'personal' force - that it cares for the individual it's in contact with. I don't think there are different forces, just one that comes dressed up differently for each group it affects. Or rather I should say that each group dresses up the force in a way that appeals to them in particular.

I think the force is 'impersonal' – just like the Force of Gravity – that it has a function to perform and has no investment or interest in the individual at a personal level. It'll show up and perform its duties wherever and whenever it's called.

2. And what calls this force into action? I believe this force shows up whenever 'any' type of symmetry has been broken and there's an honest attempt on the individual's part to restore symmetry, although probably no one but me would describe or understand it that way.

For example, let's say as a university student I had wanted to be a lawyer, and married, and successful. Those were my goals, certainly attainable, and I could honestly see my fulfillment or completion in achieving those. The symmetry of that particular situation would be restored when those goals were reached, when the picture of what I wanted matched the picture that

I got. The 'force,' always created whenever symmetry is be restored, comes into action and results either in success or failure, most often probably depending on what other goals interrupt or change the original set.

As another example, the repentant re-born Christian wants the old image of his fractured self to more closely resemble the imagined, although delusional, picture that he thinks his God has of him. He wants to reflect his willingness to be in symmetry with his God's desire. Broken symmetry, the force is activated, and it now becomes, in this instance, the Holy Spirit - although to me it's just the same old force just doing its job.

Last example - I know a young man named Jason who's having quite a time figuring things out in his life. He wants meaning and personal fulfillment and is pretty willing to reach agreement or symmetry with a correct 'final' picture. The 'force' is activated, its purpose to restore the unrealized symmetry - and fields of study like psychology and characters like Ian are introduced into his life which act as stimulants to nudge him further in the direction he himself is meant to go. Now, whether either psychology or Ian are effective or worthwhile depends on Jason's changing picture of symmetry. The force doesn't care about psychology or Ian - in fact it doesn't even care about Jason - its only aim is to achieve Jason's goal of reaching symmetry, whatever that is or whatever it becomes.

3. I also believe this force is amoral - that it makes absolutely no judgments on whether any symmetry it's trying to restore is 'good' or 'bad.' It's 'value-free' and it's faithful in performing its duty, whether it serves Hitler or Billy Graham. It is only we who differentiate between the sinners and the saints, although that judgment system needs a good revamping too.
4. If this hasn't come to your attention in the way I've set things up, Jason, then I'd better bring it up now. In the 'context' I'm describing and perhaps promoting, that if there is no 'God' as we've been programmed and conditioned to believe and if this powerful force that makes things happen is both impersonal and amoral, then the only real thing in creation that contains and emits love is us. We are the only entity in existence that cares, the only intelligence that can realize a potential. That makes what you and I are doing more important than we may already realize. In us and those like us lies the only hope for both humanity and the universe itself, and for the God that lies within us.

And that's a pretty mighty obligation, isn't it? And I thought trying to decide whether to wear blue or yellow underwear this morning would be the heaviest responsibility I'd have to handle! Right.

5. I think this force works something like the element on a stove, Jason, where it can be turned on to various degrees. Sometimes it's warm, sometimes it's hot. And I think what determines its temperature or effectiveness is the personality or type of character it's having an effect on.

The best way for me to describe this is by telling you that a characterization that holds true for me is that I've generally always been a 'dreamer.' I've always thought of questions and possibilities, I've always heavily utilized my imagination. At times I've been a poet and that role or profession is probably filled by more 'dreamers' than any other I know. And as a dreamer, I think the force worked in me only at a low temperature or speed, bringing realizations about rather slowly. Hence, my march towards my own symmetry has taken a long time, because my focus was so unclear, my gaze so far into the distance.

This has changed, I think, when 'dreams' I once had instead became 'goals.' I think the force heated up or became more active or powerful when that transition was made. I think what was happening was that my focus got closer - that goals are perhaps just dreams held at arms' length rather than over on the other side of the universe. A goal is far easier to work with than a dream. Some examples? Well, a couple of years ago, like I told you, I wanted to eliminate the various voices inside me, that never-ending internal dialogue, and turning that into a concrete goal seemed to work. There was no way I personally could have removed those voices - I knew only some other force could it. And in not trying to coerce the force into doing anything, I just focused on or set up the initial 'goal' and let the force do its work on its own. And this year I wanted to be able to be more honest and open in my life - and that goal has more than been realized in my relationship with you. I want things to matter, Jason, I want things to happen, and shifting those dreams into goals seems to enable them to become actualized.

And so I think that dedication to a goal, single-mindedness, preparedness and wholeheartedness seem to be the ingredients we need to contribute in order to have the force become more active in our lives. And

I tend to think you're better than I've been at defining goals, Jason, and I think that's why you get results and consequences far quicker than I ever did. I also think you've taught me, amongst many other things, how to do that a little better. You seem to know what you want and are pretty clear in setting it out, and so I won't be surprised at the effectiveness you'll have in getting the force to work for you.

6. The downside or drawback to strong personality types who easily create achievable goals and are therefore considered 'successful' by worldly standards is that they're often just 'materialists.' They're too concrete, have little or no real imagination, contain little love and have become virtually 'soulless.' Do you remember Jesus saying that it would be easier for a camel to pass through the eye of a needle than it would be for a rich man to enter heaven? I think he's saying they'd better start making wiser choices in the goals they set before themselves - they'd better assess things differently.

Do you think a materialist could ever create a metaphysics or valid understanding of the universe like you and I are trying to do? Not! Do you think any 'successful' person would voluntarily give up whatever god they worship? Doubtful. Have you or I ever some across an existing system that we can really value, with its multitude of gods and simple understandings? No - that's why we have to create one that we ourselves can live with, that contains elements that are important for us. And the creation of a better metaphysics is a goal, isn't it, Jason - not just a dream? That we're in a broken symmetry, and our march, with the backing or power of the universal force, will lead us to the restoration of that symmetry.

7. I think the last point I'd like to make here is to present this consideration. I believe God had to create an impersonal, amoral force that would do whatever was required to bring His people into correct relationship to themselves, which also would be how His own realization in us would come about - but this force would have to blanket all of mankind and everything man did. I think God took quite a risk in allowing that force to bring 'any' goal of man into realization - that most often, if not all the time, the goals chosen and actualized were exactly what's created the mess we've found ourselves in. Remember, in my scenario, God isn't sitting outside having an influence on anything – He's

just in our potential. The only 'thing' working in the universe is this impersonal, amoral Universal Force.

God had to hope that once in a while there'd be people dissatisfied enough to imagine new goals, there'd be people who wanted to live in a greater truth surrounded by greater love. And you and I are two such people, Jason, and I'm not too sure if what we do is 'because' of the situation or 'in spite of' the situation. Maybe it's both.

POWER; To be brief, I think power is simply the force working in one person's life coming into contact or relationship with the force (or lack of it) working in another. And since I believe the force is both impersonal and amoral, then it itself can't determine how one system will relate to the other. If there is a hierarchy involved, I think eventually the 'quality' of the goal determines which will be more 'powerful' than the other. And the 'quality' ultimately is determined by the closeness of the particular goal to our real as well as imagined potential. For example, I don't think a successful businessman could hold a candle next to a successful saint, because, at least in my mind, the saint's goals have a far higher mystical quality to them than the crass monetary goals of the businessman. The saint is 'closer' to God's original intentions than the businessman is.

Now unfortunately we don't have any living saints to test this on, although I think one is being developed in you and another one in me, so we'll personally get to test my theory. Are you scared yet?

I've never gone eight pages with you before, Jason, but I don't think it's dragged too much. Right now I feel like there's a mountain between us, built from all the words contained in all the pages and ideas I've shared with you lately. I've gotten so involved in this I can't see where you are anymore, not knowing where on the other side of this mountain you are, or if perhaps you've just wandered off.

And because I've lost sight of you, and because of the importance of the subject, I want to talk about my (or perhaps our) MISSION or DESTINY with you in person rather than on paper, OK? What exactly is it that we're here to do and how will we do it?

And I also miss you right now, Jason. I need your face and your reality in front of me in order to go further down this road, because at this point it feels too much like just a mirror in front of me - that I'm just talking to myself.

You should probably also know that what I've set before you in the last few letters I've never set before anyone before. You've enabled me to try to present my metaphysical understanding of the situation for the first time in written or recorded form, and that exercise is a valuable one. Both of us need to be able to fully express ourselves to someone capable and willing to understand, and we do that for each other. So again my thanks go your way for your ability to do that - it's something I've always needed to find in someone else and you're doing it just right.

How about a coffee or a beer or a meal together real soon? Since you seem to be carrying all the weight right now, Jason, then you're the best one to determine when you can afford the energy and time for that - so can I leave it to you to call? And as you should know, I'll always want words from you, I'll always want you to be able to come my direction with your own thoughts and ideas, your own dreams and goals.

And, damn it, I love you.

Ian

NOTES FROM THE AUTHOR

August, 2011

My original working title for this collection of letters was MINI-MOAR. I had felt that my correspondence with Jason quite represented the way I like to relate to people and since it spanned a three year time frame - it might be all you needed to gauge how I might relate to you as well. It's more-or-less me in a nut shell. MINI-MOAR. Nice.

Its sub-title had been ONE MOAR EXPLANATION - which I was using as a way of describing my metaphysical understanding about life - which you've just finished reading. But I've warmed up to the idea of just calling the whole collection ONE MORE PARADIGM – and leave it at that. Just one more to add to the pile of systems some of us invariably use, or investigate - wondering perhaps which one(s) might make most sense for we as individuals and the stories of our lives.

This collection of writing now hits a juncture, a split in the road - and I would like to describe how that split developed - silly as it seems. One road that breaks from this particular junction continues to follow my relationship with Jason, which changes drastically at this point in time. The other road breaks into some further observations of mine regarding this metaphysical understanding I've created. One road will eventually dissolve into nothingness, perhaps – and the other one you're delving into now, a never-ending cycle of amazing discoveries.

Let me take care of my relationship with Jason first. I have mentioned that he and I met for a Denny's breakfast a number of times, and the last time I ever encountered him in person was at such a breakfast. It must have happened before my two letters regarding metaphysics went his way through Canada Post, although on re-reading the series I'm thinking our last breakfast must have actually been four letters, on my part - back from here.

Our last breakfast happened on a beautiful spring day in Calgary, Alberta. The location all of our others had also. And after our typical two or three hour breakfast, we joined hundreds of strollers along the sidewalks beside the Bow River, which winds along Memorial Drive - and just across the river from downtown Calgary. A popular doughnut shop is about the only facility to offer public washrooms along the way, and after half a dozen coffees and a few glasses of water at breakfast, I needed to make a stop.

On leaving the doughnut shop Jason and I had to again cross over a four foot high bank of snow that had been created when plowing the parking lot of the doughnut shop after winter snow falls.

I can't recall if I had to actually shove Jason up and over this snow bank or simply followed him over, but I mentioned immediately that I thought he had a cute ass. Remember, I had basically only encountered him face-to-face before, either when he worked behind the Service Counter at the lumber supply store or sitting across from him at the few breakfasts we shared. Little did I know that that one comment was what would bring our relationship to a somewhat shattering close. That simple little observation of mine ended up the catalyst that wrecked what Jason and I had going for us.

Knowing that, the dramatic change in the tone of our relationship will make more sense to you. I think the text itself will more than adequately explain what ensued.

I am writing this in late August, 2011, and recently Googled Jason to see what's become of his life. He's apparently doing research for a huge, well-known American corporation and living in the States, after attaining a Master's Degree in Engineering Psychology. Never before hearing of such a degree, I thought it at first an oxy-moron, but engineering and psychology are both scientifically-based - so not necessarily as far apart as I had first imagined. After all, both are a pretty typical, left-brained, male way of handling concrete reality and the underlying mysteries that might occasionally befuddle our lives.

Of course I wonder how Jason, now in his mid-thirties, would now characterize or analyze the relationship we once had. I would also wonder how much he bought into the cultural monster or 'regular' life he was once so terrified of buying into. As you will see, he obviously made his choice to find a secure future imbedded in the structure of the established society and chose not to relate to me. Therefore, the picture that he most wanted for himself has undoubtedly come true for him - as I said it would. But I would still wonder about the longings of his soul, if they were ever genuine in the first place - or if they were easily cast aside as lucrative pay cheques were deposited in his bank account. Was he but a spiritual dilettante, unprepared and ultimately unwilling to handle the challenges of dealing with his human soul? I wonder all those things . . .

Jason once told me he intended to someday write a book - at that time the subject unknown. I suspect he's undoubtedly published some of his research papers, but perhaps the actual published book itself is still ahead of him. I had wondered when he first mentioned that goal fifteen years ago if what he wrote might be his reflections on what we discussed at those breakfast meetings, our correspondence as contained in this book, and any affects this book might have on others.

And I am even more prone to believe that happening now. After all, with a Master's Degree in Engineering Psychology, he might well straighten all of you out on what you're encountering reading this old correspondence that passed between him and me. It would undoubtedly be quite valuable to get his take on what's actually happening here from a clinical or psychological point of view. I'm sure he could help us from falling over some precipice of ill-fated belief – just more crazy meanderings from a guy like me.

METAPHYSICIAN – HEAL THYSELF!

I'd like to now turn to a deeper discussion of my metaphysical understanding of how I think life works. I have had fifteen years to watch and apply my formulation on systems I've encountered – and have yet to find something out in the world around me that my ideas don't apply to.

That's neat. Also a bit scary, perhaps - as I might have created an understanding that is beyond all present understandings of reality. No matter if it religious, spiritual or totally secular and materialistic - what perhaps ultimately makes them work 'IS' my system. It reminds me of my Microsoft Vista Operating System on my laptop - that underlies or allows the workings of any software programmes I might install.

You might be interested in this note I sent to John Horgan, a Senior Editor of SCIENTIFIC AMERICAN MAGAZINE at the time, just after I finished reading his book, THE END OF SCIENCE, in the late 1990's. Along with a few other articles of mine, I included the two letters to Jason you've just read regarding my new metaphysical understandings. Here's part of that note;

"To me, Mr. Horgan, the most significant enclosure you'll find in this package is the final one – which is the outline of my own particular philosophy or metaphysical understanding about life. I guess what has stymied and intrigued me greatly in life is the puzzle of why things seem to work the way they do. And although I'll use the idea of a 'Universal Force' in my understanding, it could also be presented in words you yourself used when defining the Copenhagen Interpretation of Quantum Mechanics: "Subatomic entities such as electrons have no real existence; they exist in probabilistic limbo of many superimposed states until forced into a single state by the act of observation."
You then mention that John Wheeler "proposed that reality might not be wholly physical; in some sense our cosmos might be a participatory phenomenon, requiring the act of observation, and thus of consciousness itself."
I think what I'm trying to say here is that, simply, when someone looks at something intently (like the Gods or value systems we choose) and wants it to become 'real' or 'true' for them, then that thing, once "existing in a probabilistic limbo of many superimposed states" is "forced into a single state by the act of observation." It becomes true and real for that person and he can hang his hat on it.
Another way to say it is that a particular religious, spiritual or secular belief has no actual truth to it until someone believes it. That while the act of someone believing in something is true, it doesn't make what is believed true. What is believed actually tells us more about the believer than the belief. The determining factor seems to be how someone becomes 'convinced' or 'certain' that a belief, understanding or value system is true.
And that's been the job of successful preachers, teachers, parents and politicians, salesmen, scientists, the arts, music and media business and that all-pervasive peer pressure throughout human history – to encourage people to 'observe' things in a particular way."

OBSERVATIONS AND APPLICATIONS

I would hope at this point that a serious reader will have applied both my own version of a working Universal Force as well as the above 'from observation to certainty to accepted truth' versions to their own particular choices and situations in life. Failure to do so would render this book entirely useless, either in its writing or its reading.

As mentioned earlier, I have watched my theory of an over-arching Universal Force for fifteen years now and haven't come across an application where it doesn't work or doesn't apply. Not to say one doesn't possibly exist - but that I haven't yet come across one. I don't care if it's some religious, spiritual or secular application – this understanding of mine seems to hold. You choose some particular system of religious or spiritual belief, accept an established working paradigm like the scientific method or even chosen beliefs like the existence of UFO's, NDE's and/or reincarnation, etc. etc. – and the Universal Force will make it 'appear' true in your life. Change your picture of understanding or belief, and that same Force will re-supply you with 'new' supporting evidence or incidents that make it again appear true. It's all relative – relative to you!

When I apply that Force to my own life, I see several things that have happened over time - and I'd like to share those with you now. I have tried occasionally over the last fifteen years to build up this Universal Force with more characteristics other than just being 'impersonal' and 'amoral' - but nothing seems to stick. And I like that, because it also keeps dogma from seeping in and making this whole contraption just one more religion.

I see though, that because this Force has granted me a continuing sense of insights and understandings about particular situations I've found myself in - that I've granted it a degree of 'caring' – which is a mistake! I think I have taken my own sense of caring about my own situation and painting that Universal Force with that characteristic. It couldn't care less and would let me colour it any shade I desired – which quickly can become a dogmatic fault.

I also see that over time it has also been difficult for me to totally erase the imbedded belief of a transcendent God who also cares for me. I suspect an early upbringing in the United Church of Canada and then two years as a heavy-duty Charismatic Christian in my mid-twenties tainted my sub consciousness into this invasive and debilitating understanding about the divine.

I have recently come to understand this error as I have gathered and re-read the material in this book. I see that the only thing or entity that really cares about me and my understandings about life - is me! Any God I imagine is only a self or man-made construct anyways – and a common one for billions of people.

PREDICTIONS, PROPHECIES AND PROGNOSTICATIONS

I recently watched a well-produced TV programme dealing with the most major problems facing mankind - a group of half a dozen experts in their specific field of study - each convincingly trying to portray his field of interest as the one that would eventually cripple our world. Over-population, food and water scarcity, peak oil, financial catastrophe, ecological degradation, magnetic shift of the poles and accompanying earthquakes, hurricanes and volcanic eruptions, and the eventual domination by highly developed computers and robots – the whole gamut of man-made craziness. Add to that the end-of-the-world prophecies of the major Judaic/Christian/ Muslim religions, meanings of the end of the Mayan calendar and other prognostications - and we have quite a contentious and threatening mix.

I can't imagine anyone reading this book not familiar with such a litany of potentialities. My contribution here is to simply suggest that these are but metaphors or frightening but easily envisioned representations of the original intent of the universe – to eventually reach its intended goal by the process of pushing the idea of symmetry to its ultimate close. To powerfully bring things back to the place before things were broken apart, that breaking point establishing the need for the Universal Force to affect symmetry. To re-establish the original state of being – although this time becoming a hologram of fulfilled or fully-completed individuals instead of just the original single entity we'd call God.

There is a greater intention at work here than the bleak forecasts so many are making - far more powerful than the measly little everyday intentions you and I might harbour. There is a greater symmetry to be restored than the more simple pictures and dreams you and I might hold.

And I'm predicting it will come to pass, just as this Universal Force shifts its allegiance from our individual intentions to its original, overriding creative intentions from the beginning of Time - the intentions that caused the formation of the Universal Force itself.

Particular things might well matter to you and me, but that is overwhelmingly overshadowed by what matters to the universe itself. Our world will ache, its people undoubtedly challenged and thrown about as the universe aligns itself with its original intentions. The most ultimate and perfect symmetry will soon be restored. The Forces that were inadvertently created to bring our universe back to its original shape and desire, will, at first, overpower us as they simply go about their job in the greatest renovation job imaginable. And then those forces will simply disappear as perfect symmetry is restored.

I somewhat suspect the universe will likely have to have another go at it, since, to me – the experiment has failed miserably this time around. It might well break apart again – needing another attempt by a re-constituted Universal Force to restore its next type of symmetry – with entities again yearning to discover their potential, re-created as new intentions and strivings of the soul of the universe - whatever it imagines and dictates. To perhaps collapse, then break apart again in order to create new or different possibilities, striving to reach its ultimate intention – to find and perfect perfect love.

Those who truly value their own souls will instinctively and intuitively understand all of this. And those who don't, will simply shudder and close down.

This week I received an email from a friend in Vancouver, he somewhat intrigued by the dire predictions of the 35,000 year old entity called Ramtha who's channelled by JZ Knight - and asked me for my own beliefs concerning the supposed end times.

In a rather sweeping generalization, and in perhaps displaying my own level of present frustration with the situation, I said; "Simply put, I think most of us are emotionally dead and spiritually inert. We devote way too much energy into tawdry, mindless distractions and endless enthusiasms. We've become metaphysically bankrupt – there's nothing in the account."

"However, I also believe that what scrapings of the human soul we might still possess - that remnant vibrates with enough real anxiety to manifest the fears it can't face. Financial meltdowns, global warming, over-population, scarcity of food and water, world-ending geological catastrophes and the prognostications of tyrants like the God of Abraham (in all 3 branches of the family – Christian, Muslim and Jewish), the implications of the Mayan calendar and characters like Ramtha and their

Armageddon-type scenarios, are, to me, but the soul's debilitating failure to pay decent attention to itself, and that failure will bring about the very disasters these scenarios envision. Nice."

"You mentioned in your email, Albert - that the world might be better off without us – but I think the world, and in fact the whole universe, was created explicitly to enable we humans to become everything we were intended to be. However, we've failed miserably at that task and I think the universe is likely ready to erase this pathetic attempt and start again in a different mode."

ON COVER ART AND ON PARADIGMS

If you look at the cover art again, you might easily relate the image and the artist's chosen title of 'E-SCAPE ... FROM COMPLEXITY' as quite fitting to the present state of the world. Everything seems to be exploding, failing to make sense and extremely discomforting for many. I believe it a very accurate portrayal of where we're at in both time and space.

Generally speaking, I believe I am an easy guy to understand – that people read my words without difficulty. I also believe my metaphysical understanding about life is the clearest and cleanest I've ever encountered. It's simple to understand, probably just as easy to apply to anyone's situation, anyone's life. What I also like is its tendency to throw off any dogma that wants to attach itself. This Universal Force is both Impersonal and Amoral and needn't be anything more. What matters most is the God that lies within our soul, wanting to express Itself to its highest degree possible in who each of us are – but will only do that if we're lined up with the original intentions and goals of the universe. The turning of mankind into loving, creative beings, filled with the energy and enthusiasm to change themselves and the world for the better.

Unfortunately, we have not reached anywhere close to the critical mass required to do anything decent. We're floundering and totally bewildered, perhaps chaining ourselves to outmoded beliefs that fail to rectify anything of intrinsic value to either ourselves or our world.

I used to hear the word 'paradigm' only in the context of a 'paradigm shift' – that is, the need to move something from one pattern of understanding to another. For example, the world theoretically has taken such a shift in its understandings about the human cause of global warming over the years.

What I am suggesting is two-fold. One is that we need to take a drastic turn, make another paradigm shift – in the way we understand the metaphysical world and how it works. And how that applies to not only our world, but more importantly – how it's supported the very choices we've personally made all the way along that have put us in the spot we find ourselves.

I think the paradigm found in these writings is just such a pattern which, if accepted and applied, would reveal both the underlying way the Universal Force has made things happen and what it intends to do now.

Secondly, a newer grasp of things already mentioned - and this is primarily a combination of Joseph Chilton Pearce's insight (see Epigraph page containing three quotations at the front of this book) of someone being an actual paradigm themselves and that odd speculation of scientist Roger S. Jones in PHYSICS FOR THE REST OF US, that I 'put on a mental shelf' in my one letter you just read to Jason - that "The world is so symmetrical in 'supersymmetry' theories that there is no distinction between the interacting and messenger particles. The particles that sense the force and the particles that transmit the force are interchangeable. In effect, there is no meaningful difference between the particles and the forces. They are one and the same."

What I'm implying here is that for the God inside us to truly immerge, then we must consciously allow that Universal Force to do its best work in us. We must choose the very best possibilities of our potential to become the picture that we want and trust that Universal Force will bring it about. But in doing so, we also likely can become that very force and so affect the world around us. For example, that is probably the guiding spirit behind the sharing of these writings to Jason, as well as the words I've formulated here. I've become that force, hoping you'll become your own expression of that very force too. I can't see any other way, quite frankly – for you to survive your own situation - no matter what it is.

Now you might get back into the story of the interactions of Jason and me. I regard it as running horizontally – just a story in time. I regard these additional sections of this book I've added for this publication as being more vertical, going down inside each and every one of you at an individual level – and therefore of higher importance. All you can likely do is make judgments about the interactions of Jason and I – but can actually gain some understandings and insights into the workings of your own life by going deep inside - or vertical.

A FEW FINAL ITEMS

I haven't the faintest idea if this book will make an impact on anybody. I would have few valued friends that I could recommend it to myself if written by someone else. I suppose I've been surprised and also disappointed in how few people I've encountered in life that truly think life is a mystery and set about finding a decent solution – or understanding. I think, instead, most people, if the least inclined in that direction, become but religious or spiritual dilettantes - soon settling for something convenient and comfortable to believe in.

The success or lack of success of this book is out of my hands. I've done what I could do – present a new way of looking at our situation. Now it would be up to the Universal Force to disperse these writings if they're anywhere important at all. And what I also like is that it puts this same Universal Force on record, I suppose forcing it to either changing its modus operandi or not. To either powerfully back the original intentions of the creator of the universe, that God that's buried within our souls – or continue to be a supposed non-factor in anything. Just backing everyone and everything - as it's done from the beginning of humanity as we know it. We either get to see the world and its populations self-destruct or be instead encouraged to actually become everything we were designed to become - although the locale or settings or type of reality might drastically change.

I don't know if this is the type of book that would become popular just by word of mouth. It certainly might if the dramatic changes I'm advocating actually begin happening – that is, support for non-aligned interests and allegiances to dwindle, those that support and encourage the development of soul to increase. It'll be an interesting year or so ahead of us all.

As to the remainder of this book – and although you may disagree with my outlook – I find my role, my interaction with Jason much like what our souls are trying to do with us. To make good contact, to show

how valuable we are at an individual level. My failure to do that with Jason might also totally reflect his soul's failure to have him pay attention to the things that really matter.

But then, that is only my perception, and Jason would certainly have and be totally entitled to his own understandings about the process or engagement we once had. Just as your perception of this collection of writings is also and only your perception. Need I make the point again that those perceptions, how we see things – colour everything we are and what we do in life? That perhaps nothing is as important as your perceptions of this whole collection – as your fate or how your world unfolds from here on out - might simply yet powerfully depend on the choices you make, the understandings you reach, the attention you pay to your soul.

My final words, then, are these;

If not you and me, then who?
If not you, then only me?
Then let it be . . . . . .

Tuesday Nov 5

Ian,

Well rather than deal with the content of your letters directly I wanted this letter to focus more on the feelings that they evoked in me (sounds kind of egocentric, doesn't it? Oh well.) I must say that it was good to hear from you after the first letter but honestly the accumulation of four letters in the last two weeks has been a little overwhelming for me. It is not to say that I don't appreciate your interest in keeping in touch with me it is just that I am finding it difficult to fully address the content of the letters and still remain focused on the other aspects of my life (ie. school). Unfortunately accompanying this situation is a whole lot of guilt because it feels as though you are putting so much time, effort and thought into this relationship and I am putting in nothing. The only thing is that I can't help it because I have stuff to do and things on my mind. Although it may not seem important to you in the long run, my school is very important to me and it is hard for me to divide my thoughts between these two important aspects of my life. Hopefully you will be able to understand this and hopefully not expect as much in return.

The second thing in this letter I wanted to address was what you wrote in your second letter regarding your love for me. I just want to let you know that for me this is a very special word and although it is nice to know that you feel comfortable with me and us to feel this, I do not feel the same comfort level. It is perhaps because for me I have always associated love with intimacy and although I know that it doesn't interest me, I am not completely sure whether it doesn't interest you. This last part really scares me because it is a feeling that I have had ever since you commented on how nice my ass was the last time we got together. It really made me feel uncomfortable and honestly I closed right up after that (I'm not sure if you noticed?). The thing I don't understand is that before you said it you commented on how inappropriate you knew it was but you said it anyway. Why? What sort of thoughts did you think it would conjure up in me?

I think it is pretty obvious and in light of that you did it anyway. Why? Another one of the thoughts that came rushing to mind when you wrote about your love for me was how you described to me about how you explored the sexual identity of some of your lovers. Well I think that is great but I feel that although you are not doing it directly you are somehow trying to exercise this on me. I am not trying to say that I don't think sexual exploration isn't important, I just wanted you to know that it is not an aspect of our relationship that I want to become apparent. I just realized that this whole blurb has been focused on the assumption that you are thinking of me in an intimate way when you say that you love me. Perhaps this is a really BIG assumption on my part and I am simply jumping to conclusions - but the possibility exists and it frightens me, making this feeling of mine very difficult to ignore. All I want is a little more clarification on your part and I will try my best not to let my socialized view "that two men can't love each other without it being some sort of homosexual relationship" get in the way of my judgment. I mean I know that if I didn't know you were gay (like if you were married to a woman and had kids for example) and told me that you loved me it wouldn't bother me. So why does it bother me now? I really am not quite sure, probably mostly out of fear of the unknown. Personally, homosexuality is something I know very little about but don't entirely feel comfortable discussing with you yet. So a little more clarification on your part would be much appreciated and I will try to keep my mind clear of any conclusive thoughts.

The final thing I wanted to address and perhaps the most important is that a few days ago I ran into a young man from Cochrane that I hadn't seen in a very long time (several years). Anyways when we discussed some of the things that were new in his life he mentioned the fact that he had met an interesting man in town and that he went out for coffee with him. I asked him about this man and what he was like and guess what? - it was you! I asked him what he looked like and what the phone number was that this person had given him but most importantly he told me that this fellow was gay. So even before I had confirmed it with matching the phone numbers I had a pretty good idea that it was you. After having established that, I asked him what sort of things you talked about and his reply is what bothers me the most out of all. He says that he somehow got the impression that you were married and had kids; and I thought " What? Ian doesn't have kids, he isn't married - what the hell is going on?"

After a little further probing he also said that he remembers you clearly telling him that you had a nice sports car, a speed boat, a fishing boat, as well as other things. This kind of made we wonder if indeed we were talking about the same person but there was no denying the matching of the phone numbers. I was very confused because although we were talking about the same person it didn't seem like we knew the same person, there were so many different characteristics and inconsistencies. I just wanted to know that even if this stuff is true, how come it never got brought up in any of our discussions. It seems clear to me that something like that would have been brought up eventually (especially since we have talked about motorbikes and cars are tied right in with them). So it makes me ask, were you lying to him? Or have you been lying to me? Do you show people different sides of yourself on a regular basis? Am I seeing the real side? Was he? What is the real side? Either way it would upset me because it goes against everything that we have ever talked about. For example, stuff like being true to yourself and others around you has always been a focal point in many of our conversations. Now it doesn't seem that you honestly believe it or practice it in everyday life. Needless to say I am full of questions that are screaming for answers but rather than ask them I would like you to explain this situation and what happened. Without a doubt this has further weakened my level of trust with you because although this is all speculative it has raised many doubts and hesitancy. I know that this letter may appear rather confrontational, but it really isn't meant to be. It is more of a way of asking for clarification because without adequate clarification I don't think this level of communication between us can continue.

Jason

Tuesday, November 12th

Jason;

I've got to be in one of the oddest dispositions I've ever found myself in, and I also feel pretty mean. I wondered if I should wait before replying to your recent letter, knowing it might be a little unwise to speak out when I'm so upset. Your letter, though, was in earnest, and I believe you expect and deserve a prompt reply. I also know I'll be too busy for the next three days and unable to respond then. And by the time this weekend rolls around, I honestly wonder if I'd even care to respond. So, all in all - these old keys are getting their pounding on now, the risk of a hot-under-the-collar response accepted.

Do you remember me telling you how nervous I was on receiving your first letter, Jason? This last letter is the one where that feeling would have been more applicable. I felt blindsided, a hit from an unexpected direction. And I should probably assume that this letter of mine to you will enable you to share that wonderful experience.

If you'll forgive me for starting my response to you with a story, I'd like to tell you of a comment I made to my last lover on our first date. I said that we'd better enjoy the level of honesty a new relationship afforded, because it undoubtedly wouldn't be long before we got to know each other, and from that point on would have to more closely navigate our interactions, learning the in's and out's of how each other accepted, handled or responded to things. We'd start putting up directional signs, in effect saying that this particular item ought probably to be handled this way, that particular item handled that way. Our honesty would become personalized or subjective, and this process was perhaps inevitable and unfortunate.

Perhaps needless to say, that's exactly what happened. And while I might entertain the notion that it became just a self-fulfilling prophecy, I put more weight on it just being my understanding of how relationships tend to change shape, taking on the contours of the particular personalities of the characters involved.

I'm saying this, Jason, because I see I should have started putting up signs about things for you a while ago - but I got so caught up in what I was doing that I couldn't see where you were in it all, although I've made that admission to you several times, wanting your input, wanting you to tell me where you were. Which now you've done, with a vengeance.

One of the warning signs I should have pinned to your wall regarded the intensity of my response to you.

I should have been able to see how all the heavy shit I was dumping in your lap would have to fight for space and attention with your schooling. I should have been smart enough to either postdate everything so letters would arrive at your door two months apart, or perhaps just back out and leave you alone until you had the time and space and interest to be involved.

I do know that what I've written to you could only have been written to you then - that I couldn't begin to duplicate it now. And that was important for me to be able to do, and I've told you many times how grateful I am to you for allowing me to share those things with you.

Perhaps one section of that sign would have let you know that that pace could not be maintained - it was too dynamic. Perhaps another part should have directed you to just try to put it all on some closet shelf where it could be brought out at a more appropriate time. Perhaps the sign should have told you that you'd have the freedom to also dump them in the garbage. Perhaps the sign could have told you that I was trying to get a lot of things in before the climate changed, before the storm clouds grew. Perhaps the sign should have mentioned that Ian may never be able to respond that way again to you, either fortunately or unfortunately.

And when I sat for an hour this afternoon, reading your letter and licking my wounds, I realized I'd get shit from you either way I go. I have the space and the energy right now to devote quite a bit of time to you - but you don't need that attention now. I also know that in the future will undoubtedly come times when you'll want that attention - but chances are good my energy will be channeled elsewhere. It's kinda like you're getting what you don't want now, but may not get what you want later. And either way, I'll probably get blamed.

Anyways, I apologize for the amount of stuff I've made you handle. I never expected you to feel guilty about responding or holding up 'your end' of the relationship - just your willingness to read and think about things was all that I wanted. Guilt is not a big part of my being, and I failed to read how big an item it apparently is in you.

But you'll get what you want - lots of breathing room. I'm going to back off quite a ways, letting you determine and decide exactly what it is you want. At some future point I suppose I'd also get to choose my own response to whatever 'new' position you land in - that the situation at hand will have changed.

In hindsight, I could probably tell you that I must have subconsciously known that this junction would be reached and that I'd better take advantage of the situation before it changed - that I'd better say all the best things I could say before the limitations and restrictions went up.

And so, sort of an answer to the part of your letter where you discussed how much you had to handle right now - just breath a sigh of relief, Jason - I won't be bothering you again without an invitation.

Part Two; In your last sentence of your second letter to me, Jason, you said that "wanted to get together for a real discussion about life and to unravel more layers of our relationship." Here again I have to tell you that I'm neither a mind-reader nor omniscient - I have no idea what all the ingredients and ramifications of our relationship are - that's why any 'unraveling' we'd do would be excursions into new territory.

And the most difficult aspect, it seems, revolves around issues of love and sexuality. No matter where else those paths of discovery led, I knew beyond a shadow of a doubt, the issue of homosexuality would have to be maturely handled. It still does.

You seem to have an extraordinary number of fears in you, Jason, and perhaps could give some therapist years of work trying to unravel them. Perhaps you over-respond to particular things, while I under-respond to them - I don't know. Anyways, one of your first admitted frights was when I told you I was gay.

In my trying to help you understand the situation a little more completely, I need to hang another sign on the wall. This sign should read that I was scared at that time too. Naturally I was concerned about rejection, but my more pointed fear was that I was scared you might be gay. I would probably want to refrain from saying this to you, Jason, but you seem hell-bent on knowing the truth about everything - and I'll oblige you. From my experience and observations about people in life, I figure there's a 50/50 chance you're gay. There's also a 100% chance you wouldn't know that or accept it.

And quite frankly, I didn't want to accept it either. The last thing I'd want to do is spend my energy helping you prove or disprove that. There's no way I wanted to see you go spinning into space following that trail. That's part and parcel of me intentionally not wanting to love you, Jason - I just didn't want to go through that shit. If you were gay, I didn't want to be part of your struggle in coming to terms with that.

Now my first impression of you perhaps being gay might be completely wrong - I'll be the first to admit that. But we were both frightened - you were scared of me 'being' gay - I was scared that you 'might be' gay. Neither of us needed the shit that that subject brought. And it looks like it might be too big for us work around - or work through. It looks like it might be the thing that destroys our relationship, since you want me to be unreal in handling it and I want you to get real.

You were right about a couple of things regarding my 'you've got a cute ass' comment, Jason. I indeed did fail to see you 'close up' in reaction to it - and I also failed to empathize with how you'd feel about it. I guess I need to learn how to just stay in neutral gear, have nothing going on inside me, just so I can adequately interpret and respond appropriately to the wonderful, deserving beings around me. I think not – if you're on some 'honesty kick' here, Jason - you should accept some responsibility at not informing me immediately that you had closed down and what was going on inside you. Again, I'm no fucking mind-reader.

I doubt if I said that that comment would be inappropriate. I think I would have said that it 'might' be inappropriate, because that type of comment needs that type of hedge. And granting my error or inability to see how negatively it affected you, my own understandings would be these;

- it might have been inappropriate because you were just about to start your answer about God perhaps having a mission for you. My 'comment' would be out of joint with that.
- it might have been inappropriate because you had never heard that comment from anyone before, much less from someone whose sexual advances you'd deplore. You question my motives in saying that to you and my disregard for how you'd react to it. That's right on. But now you want to force me to 'close down' - you want me to be unreal, you want to strip away my humanity by disallowing me to make physical comments.

- I am continually surprised at the failure of people to say positive, obvious thing about those they know. I imagine if you listed the good things I've said about you in person and in my letters, the count would be quite high. If some girl who you valued asked you whether or not you knew that you had a cute ass, would you have closed down then? My comment might have been inappropriate because I'm not allowed to make comments about certain things I see, even though the same thing said by 'appropriate' others would be accepted for the compliment it is. Gee, Jason - I don't know if I'm supposed to apologize for being observant, truthful, or gay - or maybe all three. Maybe what I need to apologize for is just being me - that'll cover any other inappropriate things I might say. Maybe we should just write off Ian's humanity and instead just play with words and ideas. That's safer - and God knows we all want to be safe.

Two other items you've mentioned regarding sexuality deserve comments from me. You are under the illusion that I 'explored the sexual identity of some of my lovers' - that sounds like a psychological analysis. What I said was that my love for them precipitated a personal transformation that altered their accepted reality about themselves in a major way. I was not trying to make anyone 'gay' - but somewhere in the dynamics of our relationship we discovered that we could quite easily physically love each other, confronting the bugaboos society had about it.

In regards to this, I'm enclosing an 'addition' to one of those newspaper letters regarding homosexuality I sent you two or three weeks ago. I see that I never did give some insights of mine about why Christians always go crazy about queers, but I think it's important.

Secondly, you want to know if I want to be intimate with you. This is a bit of a dilemma for me - but I'll try to be as clear as I can. Jason - you're not my type. There are certain physical characteristics I'm attracted to, rightly or wrongly - and you don't have them. I'd never cross the room to hustle you or make any attempts to seduce you. Now that's hard for me to say. I don't like most of the things I'm saying in this letter - and I think that's about the meanest. I can't tell you not to take that personally, because that's the only way it could be taken. But I think you need a clear answer.

The dilemma, however, is this. If I wanted, I could have sex every night of the week with someone my 'type.' I could be in an intimate, full-time relationship with someone my 'type.' But I've never found, and suspect I'd never find, the qualities in them that I find in you, Jason. I can get the body, but not the being.

What I'd like to find, of course, is someone who'd be just my type as well as being just like you. I suppose I'll have to settle for a compromise, with the split - each separate and alone. But I think that you're sensing that dilemma, Jason, and your negative reaction is acknowledged. Remember that I told you that I had to give you the space to go negative on me - and I can't fault you for doing that. But the dilemma is still there, and you've made the pressure known. Again, if you want to pull the plug because you can't live with that tension - then so be it. I'm not here to fight anybody, leastwise you.

Part Three; I've had coffee with two young men in Cochrane. Two weeks ago, a young man named Paul called me as he said he would and we had a quick, three-quarter hour coffee. The conversation was really pretty shallow - he not even stumbling or showing any emotion whatsoever when recalling his grandfather dying in his arms a year earlier. I would be surprised if Paul was the fellow you mentioned, because the level he's able to attain is trivial, and if you're trying to make me compete with him for your attention - then you disappoint me.

I would hope the other fellow, Noel, is who you are talking about, because he has a lot more qualities going for him that I think both you and I admire. We actually got together twice, probably for a total of about five hours.

Noel and I actually talked about a wide range of things, and it started at a fairly superficial level. I learned, after we became comfortable with each other, that for two years (actually until his son was born this spring) he was part of a small vigilante group, likened to Guardian Angels, where their martial arts and dedication to truth and justice would enable them to 'clean up' society. Now I'm politically, intellectually and morally opposed to any such movement - so further discussions, at least on my part, were somewhat guarded. In fact, it's much like your issues with me lately - there's just a cloud over it that makes it difficult to handle cleanly.

But I'll tell you Jason, Noel is a pretty neat character - I could see he and you being good friends. And I think it was in the last hour together (he's moved into Calgary) that I mentioned my sexuality. Remember, here's a guy who'd been ready to seriously pound in a few people's heads - and in good old repressed Alberta, I can imagine any self-righteous vigilante group would have homosexuals pretty high on their list for elimination.

However, one of Noel's two best friends is gay, had been kicked out of his house, worked Calgary streets as a male prostitute until Noel pulled him off - and who is now living in the gay community of Vancouver. So Noel knew what was up, and he made things really easy to handle. I hope to spend time with him in the future - but he had jobs to find, a fiancé and baby to support.

Now if I recall, I think during my first discussion with him I mentioned my boats, because I was talking about how obsessed a young friend up at the lake became about them. The basis of our relationship had shifted from friendship to simply his use of my boat - and I thought that was a shame.

Noel would have been wrong about me having a sports car, though. Granted, most cars I've had in my life have been nice. I always thought that if I had to work at jobs I hated, then at least the money I made would pay for something I enjoyed. But that all ended when I turned forty. My last nice car was more or less repossessed. I just stopped making payments on it - and stopped using it.

But I do own a 1978 Toyota station wagon, Jason - that sits up at the Shuswap, tires probably flat, warding off any inquisitive house burglars that might boat by.

But I do remember saying something about cars that made Noel pay attention. At our first meeting, when we were sitting at an outdoor table at a coffee bar, a nice Oldsmobile Aurora pulled up and parked in front of us. I think Noel was just finishing up his 'back to the land-type' speech, when I said that if I had to get from any point A to point B, I'd rather drive a quality vehicle like the one parked in front rather than the one I had (my station wagon). I think he couldn't believe it - here he was talking about the values he held dear, and I got materialistic on him. But I told him I admired much of what man has created, and a quality vehicle like the one before us was alright by me. And he, seemingly not too interested in cars, would have looked at that $45,000 Aurora and undoubtedly thought it a sports car.

And if he had the impression I was married with kids, then that impression was strictly his. Good God, Jason, I'm not the stereotypical gay male most heterosexuals love to hate. I'm good with people and kids, people like me, and quite frankly, guys like Noel (and maybe even you) probably project their father fantasies onto me. I'm old enough to be their father, young-acting and alive enough to be their friend.

But it all gets back to those layers we mentioned before, Jason. I gravitate to whatever level a person can comfortably handle and levels handled with either Paul or Noel can't compare in depth to the level I reach with you.

But I'm sorry for not talking about cars and boats and stuff like that with you. Last Sunday morning while in Calgary, I scouted out a 1995 Corvette, a 1997 Audi A4, and that 1997 Dodge Dakota pick-up truck I mentioned to you that Sunday. Someday I want to buy all three, and if you want to come with me while I pick them up, or if you ever want to use or borrow them - then that's alright by me.

But Jesus, Jason - you could probably put everything I own inside that crappy old Toyota station wagon of mine - I'm really quite surprised how upset you got over my possessions. I'd give everything to you in a second (and that's about all the time it'd take!) if they mean that much to you - because they really don't mean that much to me.

You wonder how many 'sides' I have. I'd call them levels, and I reach different levels with different people. If the only side you value is the one I show to you - then you'd better realize I'd have to have gone fifty years without relating with anyone else until I found you. I've been more than clear with you about why I cherish the relationship you and I have - that I've never been able to duplicate with anyone else in my life. Does that make how I've had to relate to others disingenuous? Jason, you're the one who must think that how I relate to others goes against everything that we have ever talked about, because that's not what I think we've 'always' talked about. I've hold you I've wanted to be more open and honest with people, but it's situational. And if you can relate to everyone else exactly the same way you relate to me, then you're either a liar or actually have few friends or people that you do talk to.

Using your argument, should I suppose you stand up in every psychology class and state your disagreements about psychology and then share with them your truth and your 'real' reality? When you get poor service in a restaurant, do you immediately take steps to practice your high level of honesty with the waitress or manager? When you see that you don't think like everyone around you, are you kind enough to let them know that?

Do you want me to send you a list, with my name as the first signature, of those who know that Ian is not an ideal human being? And could I send you another list, again with my name as the first signature at the top, of those who suspect that Ian would indeed like to be better than he is, who's sorry that he not, and just hope to hell he doesn't get spotted, nabbed and executed by those who've already reached perfection - I guess by someone like you.

Jason, you had just so much passion in your letter - you had so much raw anger - that I've responded in kind. I don't know if we have to occasionally blow out our ballasts or what, but what a fucking ride we give each other.

You know, kid, you're teaching me to be more honest with others - that's an ongoing process. I'd sure like you to quit marking me, though, because all you seem to give me is F's. And quite honestly, I don't think you yet have the range to be able to fairly assess how I relate to others. I know you're mad at me. I just don't know if you'll use that anger, however justified or righteous – to end our relationship. That too, is your decision.

I should probably drop a prophecy into your lap right now, Jason. The day I get to be everything I am, to be whatever type of person you perhaps have 'idealized' - then that will be the day that the world will shudder. Many, many people at that time will only hope that I could be less real, less powerful, more like I am now. I guess I wonder what tune you'll play then, Jason.

Anyways, I'm tired, I'm going to bed. Wake me up if you want to continue a relationship, Jason. I'm too bagged and disappointed to fight.

Ian

Tuesday, Nov. 19th

Jason;

Well, I've woken up, smelled the coffee and realized I don't like the smell of it, Jason. I did a pretty heavy number on you in my last letter and it's taken a week for the dust to settle. Letting you alone decide whether or not our friendship is over is more than any one person ought to bear - and it is perhaps unforgivable that I've shouldered you with that responsibility.

Now I don't know if you have a letter streaming my way at this point, whether you've just simply thrown in the towel altogether, or are just waiting to see how things feel in time - but I thought it proper for me to address these words to you.

It probably would be good for both of us if you shared with me how you've been affected by the latest turn in our relationship. I would imagine in ways I hurt you quite badly - and you should unleash some of your fury at me.

I was wondering if you might want to know why I was so upset when I last wrote to you - and so describing my state of mind to you at that time is what this particular letter will be about.

Initially let me tell you that the vision I had in my head last week was that our friendship was hanging by a thread. You yourself said something similar in your own letter, saying; "Without a doubt this has further weakened my level of trust with you . . ." I thought it wise for me to throw a few stout lines your way, hoping you'll decide to hold on to them. There is so much weight on each side of our friendship that a single thread can't hold for long and I've got to actively and purposefully bolster that remaining life-line between us. Now whether or not I'm successful is another matter - but you're too important in my life, Jason - for me not to at least try.

Initially it is important for me to say that although my letter to you was in direct reaction to the letter of yours I'd just received - that your letter was entirely justified. In it you told me where you were at the time and what problems you were encountering. You latched onto and shared three areas of real concern in your life - 1) The amount of time and energy our friendship was stealing from your schooling. 2) Your valid concerns about my love for you and any possible sexual overtones. 3) Your discomfort with how you see me relating to other people. And when I look at my response to your letter, I also have to acknowledge that it too was justified. I think I gave you some pretty clear answers to the questions you had.

But now, a week later - I see some of the damage that was caused by that exchange - and thought I'd better try to mend a few fences. What saddens me, however, is the possibility that we've crossed some line that keeps us both from going back or from going forward. About three years ago, at a time of extreme stress for both of us, my sister and I had a major confrontation - and even though it blew itself out and we can be serene with each other - it has still left its dark mark. We may never recover completely from it and if possible, Jason - I'd like to prevent that from happening between you and I.

And so, let me tell you why I was so pissed off last week.

1. As you know, or as you've experienced, I've done a fair amount of writing over the years. I think I've reached levels of understanding in very particular areas that I'll probably never surpass, and have been able to get those insights decently down on paper. Henceforth, if someone needed my views on abortion, on politics, on intellectuality, on discrimination, on health or on a few other subjects that don't immediately come to mind - then I could just have them read the appropriate piece of writing. I regard those writings, rightly or wrongly, as being sufficiently powerful and encompassing and do not need further words on my part. My position on those subjects was both exhaustive and definitive - that I don't think I could get to a much simpler understanding or one that went beyond my present understanding.

I'm saying this, Jason, because the letter I sent to you just before your last letter to me was one such letter. Now you may never realize this, and I can't fault you for it - but that letter about the hidden force of the universe, was a very important and very powerful letter. In the years to come, that particular letter will be something I can stand on as I fight my way through the mystery I'm enmeshed in.

When that particular letter went your way, I couldn't imagine how you could respond to it - other than just critiquing it. And so, when I got your last letter, that's what I was expecting - some particular response of yours to a very important position of mine. That's why I was so unprepared, so blind-sided by the letter of yours that I actually got.

2. I was upset at myself for never giving you the break you really needed from all my shit in order for you to responsibly handle your schoolwork. I'm really sincere in saying I wish I could have found a more appropriate way to relate to you so that you could juggle two very important things in your life, your 'inside' and your 'outside' worlds, in a less stressful manner.
3. Perhaps the two most important aspects of my life have been my sexuality and my spirituality. I regard you, Jason, as having deep and powerful connections to my spiritual side and would probably like to leave it that way. But I've got so much history in my life regarding sexuality that I have been unable to keep that shadow from creeping over you. And I don't know what to do about it except acknowledge it. I do know that my sexuality and spirituality are so entwined that they can't be separated, something most spiritually developed people acknowledge. But you know when that shadow has crossed over you, Jason - and that has made you uncomfortable. Again, I can't save you from that - but I certainly can acknowledge and respect your discomfort. Simultaneously, you need to know I won't repress my sexuality any more than I'll repress my spirituality with you, Jason - and can only ask you to tell me immediately when you're bothered. Actually, I hope we can reach the stage where we'll allow humor to help us through it.
4. I was upset by how upset you became over how I relate to others. If anything, I thought you'd be jealous if you discovered that I interacted with others exactly like I do with you - instead you were upset because I didn't. Jason, you're really special to me and God only knows how I wish I could relate to everyone exactly like I relate to you - and someday I hope I get closer to being able to do that. But right now that's a long ways off, and the situation itself helps dictate it.

Secondly, I was a little disturbed about the superficial things you and this other person talked about. He seemed to have started that part of your conversation by saying he had met an 'interesting' man in Cochrane, but rather than going into why he thought I was 'interesting,' you guys instead went elsewhere. I think that if that other fellow had a five minute quiz on why he thought I was 'interesting,' impressions of my marital status, my possessions or anything else of that sort would never be mentioned. I would suggest that I'm interesting because of my 'depth' - not my 'shallowness.'

And I couldn't quite figure why you went down that pathway with him, Jason? It surprised me, and it actually disappointed me. But then, I've disappointed you more than enough to make up for that - just in case it's a contest!

And someday, maybe way off in the future, I'd sure like to know these things about you, Jason, things that particular letter of yours perhaps uncovered;

– I can't imagine what would motivate me to interact at a serious level with fellow human beings if I didn't love them. If you make a direct connection between love and intimacy, what is it that you figure motivates you to have any interest at all in those around you? Is it intellectual curiosity or what? - and will it supply you with the amount of motivation you'll need to do the deeds you need to do? I'd like to understand that about you.
– you've told me that you've discovered that you think differently from those around you - and I want to know what that's all about. I now realize that I really don't understand what you actually mean when you say that you don't think the same way they do. I guess I just made the presumption that your experience was like mine - but it may not be.

Can I give you an example of where someone thinks differently from those around him - and is it kind of like the difference you feel? And although this example is of a 'physical' nature - I don't mean that that has to apply in any way to your situation.

Example; My last intimate encounter involved someone almost exactly like myself. Although younger, at 36 - he was quite good looking, a really nice guy, has been teaching high school for twelve years. He mentioned that he just 'came out' to his mom this past Easter, doesn't know if he'll ever be able to confront his dad. He's finally found a good few friends in the last year and feels more comfortable with who he is. Now he had a really hairy body, like I do, but he shaves the hair on his back and is hopeful no one will deride him for it.

What was a little funny is that I mentioned that with the amount of hair he had on his body that he should be thankful he had such a good head of hair. I told him I myself went bald in my early twenties. Maybe you've guessed it - but somewhere during the night I inadvertently ran my hand across the top of his head and discovered he was wearing a wig. I don't think he realized I knew - but it made me empathize for him. I remember trying a wig for a month or two in my early twenties and knew the anxieties it also produced.

So here was a guy handling things like I did at a little more than half his age. And I thought I'd been a late bloomer, taking longer than I ought to have in maturely taking care of those awesome anxieties. Here was a 36 year old man who's yet to be honest with both parents, who's just recently found friends and harbors high anxiety about his body and his baldness. He's 36 and not allowed himself to be real yet - most things are still a cover-up.

Anyways, I bet if I asked him if he's figured he's thought like others at any time of his life, including now - I bet he'd answer 'no.' His differences, I would suggest, resulted from tremendous anxiety as well as an undeveloped or immature ability to get honest with himself, while everyone around him had more easily been able to do that.

And I'm wondering what your differences are, Jason? Are you behind others or ahead of them or just somewhere completely different? And I'm not expecting an answer now, because I know you're trying to find the answers yourself. I just want to get myself out of the assumption that your differences might be similar to mine - although they still might be. Anyways - a mystery.

Sometime in the future, if we're still connecting, I want to talk to you about fears you have about future confrontations we'll face with others and the world around us. Your fears in that department are just as legitimate as your other fears, and we need to spend some time acknowledging and dealing with them. I figure what I'm going to be doing in the world will be scary, and I suspect that what you'll be doing will be scary too - and we should talk about it.

But in closing, I'd like to explain the dichotomy I believe we've been caught in, Jason. On the one hand, I think we're both trying to push Maslow's self-actualizing characteristic of adopting the 'I don't give a shit' attitude you mentioned a little too far - where we don't allow ourselves to be influenced by each other. Our last letters to each other are examples of our attempts to succeed at this - and it can be a pretty miserable process.

U.B.C. Psychologist Paul Trapnell, in researching certain types of behavior, speculates "that one of the reasons 'disagreeable' men, described as manipulative, arrogant, boastful and calculating - get the most sex is because they don't care who they hurt. They go after what they want, and don't worry about the consequences."

"Unfortunately though it may be," he continues, "ruthlessness is the key to success in many fields besides sexual conquest. It seems to me that just about anybody hungry for success might reach the top faster if they didn't lose any sleep over a little manipulation."

I guess what I'm trying to say here, Jason - is that my own 'attitude in your face,' as recorded in my last letter, needs refinement, if not total elimination - when I relate to you.

The other end or side of this dichotomy, and the actual thing that prompted me to write this letter, is reflected in this quotation from UNCONDITIONAL LIFE by Deepak Chopra;"'I live in another dimension,' she mourns. This persistent feeling of isolation makes things very fearful for her. She has no security. The rest of us are at home; she is the eternal stranger."

"Many sensitive people feel this way. Wisdom and poetry can arise from this situation as easily as anguish. But given how lonely such people generally are, I can see why anguish is the most common response. It is by relating to other people, after all, that most of us manage to feel real in the first place."

I could be wrong here, Jason, but I sense you and I, in trying to be as 'upfront and honest' as we think we ought to be with each other, are risking ending up at the other extreme - isolated, alone and in anguish. The last person I want out of my life is you, and without being dishonest, will try my best at really respecting who you are, who I am, and how to best deal with our realities and what we're here to do.

I think of you sometimes and my heart almost breaks - but more often I'm enthused and excited about who we are and where we're going. I hope what we have hasn't been ruined.

Ian

Ian Moar
*** Christleton Ave.
KELOWNA, B.C.

Sept. 5th, 1997

Jason;

I won't try to be light-hearted by simply asking how you are, Jason - there's far too much water under the bridge between us to pretend that we can be superficial with each other. I'm somewhat amazed that almost a year has passed since I last saw you - and so I do wonder who you are now and how you really have been doing?

I need to tell you at the outset of this letter that I never expected to get to know someone like you in my life - and all the things that transpired between us were therefore unexpected too. Although I usually don't have problems putting down what I want to say - I'm somewhat caught at not knowing how to describe the appreciation I have for both the challenges you've given me and the positive affect you've had on my life. No one has taken me the distances you have, Jason. No one has encouraged me to delineate or outline in words so many of the important things that I feel - and you need the acknowledgment for doing all of that.

The way in which the relationship between us folded also reflects how my significant relationships seem to come to an end - and I'd like to say a thing or two about that. I used to think that I was just too awkward a character for others to handle well - that I challenged them in ways that became too difficult for them to bear. A lady I know sees how easy it is for people to reject me because I apparently 'scold' everyone - which she says no one will tolerate. Both of these understandings or rationalizations make sense - and perhaps you have an insight or two of your own to add, Jason.

Recently, though, I've been looking at this 'problem' from another perspective - which I'd like to share with you because I think it stems from the particular relationship that you and I once had. You, however, may well think it's total bullshit.

Anyways, several weeks ago, in the middle of the night, I was able to finally verbalize my main goal in life - one I've been striving and struggling to find, understand and then articulate since I was your age. Simply put, 'MY GOAL IS TO CREATE A CONSCIOUS WORLD THAT I CAN LIVE IN COMFORTABLY.' Once set down, once infused with personal meaning and heartfelt passion, I also knew this is what the dynamic energy force of the universe needed in order to become activated.

As I peer at this 'goal' from various angles, marveling at both its apparent simplicity and underlying levels of complexity, I must also acknowledge that this 'goal' is probably the goal of the universe itself. I imagine that the whole shebang was created in order that we might 'create a conscious world that we all could live in comfortably.' Even your own struggles, Jason, probably revolve around your heart-felt desire to be comfortable in your own situations.

Now this also helps me come to grips with understanding what's happening with mankind. I have always known that we were at a pivotal stage in history - but I needed to know why it was pivotal and what exactly would instigate the types of formidable changes I believe will presently beset us. Christians who are worth their salt all believe we're in the 'endtimes' - but they never seem able to explain why this particular point in history is any more significant in specific terms than any other. There also seems to be an abundance of 'metaphysical seekers' in the world today who intuitively sense the need for a profound change in the way we exist. And then there are particular characters like you, Jason, who just seem to feel a general unease in the way most things transpire, and who yearn to have things make a better type of sense.

When I turn around and assess my personal relationship with you, Jason, I feel sad, disappointed and angry with myself for the way I let it unravel. I also feel sad, disappointed and angry at you for the part you yourself played. Furthermore, I feel sad, disappointed and angry at our shared situation in general - pissed off at the seemingly built-in impossibility of our relationship developing further than it did.

And that whole idea of being sad, disappointed and angry at ourselves and the situation not only is the most appropriate response for us but might also be the exact response required to move mankind out of its present malaise and into a more mature, more developed stage. And since I don't believe in a God like we've been conditioned to believe, then I can't say that He is sad, disappointed and pissed off at mankind and is going to finally make a move against it - like most serious Christians believe. Instead, those exact feelings have to be sincerely felt at some individual level - by us - by you and me and all those others who seek a more meaningful and rewarding existence.

Our destiny, our mission, then, would be to bring that about - to let that festering sadness, disappointment and anger loose on the world, releasing the energy to change life as we know it in a dramatic and beneficial way. And so, if I thought I made people reject me because of my 'awkwardness' or 'scolding,' I now see that it'll probably only get worse, as I direct the sadness, disappointment and anger from doing damage to me internally - to venting it externally, where it rightfully belongs.

Three quotations from three different authors perhaps take us to the same assessment, although mainly of Western culture;

1. Thomas Moore, in CARE OF THE SOUL; "'Psychological modernism' is an uncritical acceptance of the values of the modern world. It includes blind faith in technology, inordinate attachment to material gadgets, uncritical acceptance of the march of scientific progress, devotion to the electronic media, and a life-style dictated by advertising. This orientation toward life also tends toward a mechanistic and rationalistic understanding of matters of the heart."
2. Deepak Chopra, in UNCONDITIONAL LIFE; "The only way out of Maya is to wake up from its spell, to join the few who are not truly enchanted. In our culture, the spell has become respectable as 'hard' science, but that does not make it truer. The advantage of seeing through Maya is that the scientific spell, although it has given us this convenient modern life with its jets and computers, CAT scans and carrot juicers, has not done away with fear, violence, hatred and suffering. Those have been programmed into Maya too. They come with this dream when you agree to be its dreamer."
3. David Ehrenfeld, in BEGINNING AGAIN; "The late Jesuit scholar Pierre Teilhard de Chardin foresaw the day when all human consciousness would flow together into one great unified layer, becoming part of the "noosohere" and enveloping the earth in its collective and spiritual wisdom. Have we moved, or are we moving, in that direction? I think not!"

I should probably also say, Jason - that all of humanity needn't agree with any of this. Perhaps those who don't will simply be left behind.

Now when I think of you, Jason, and how all this fits together, I have to say that I believe you have an important function to perform. You're someone that will also make things happen, but it will likely necessitate you making a major decision at some point. I believe I once told you that one purpose of me being in your life was in order to comfort you if you ever came to a crossroads - where you had to decide to continue on the main road or break off and follow a path that had only your name on it. I also suggested you might well be a 'soul' doctor, and those two ideas perhaps perfectly describe the dilemma you'll have to handle - or may be handling now.

Thomas Moore, in CARE OF THE SOUL, also says that; "Psychology is a secular science, while care of the soul is a sacred art." I'm thinking, Jason, that at some point in time you're going to have to choose between which type of doctor you want to be - one who operates out of his head or one who operates out of his heart. One who supports and defends the 'status quo' or one who revolutionizes how mankind lives. And since, to me, you seem to be such a concoction of both elements - that it'll perhaps have to be the situation at hand which forces or determines the direction you'll go. I also suggest that world or social changes will sweep you in the direction of following your heart, which will mean traveling down your own road. But that perhaps comes directly from my own longings - and I know what you might feel about that.

I want you to know, Jason, that I'm not intentionally trying to kick-start our relationship again. I know you're at school and I know you're doing the things that you feel are most important for you to do. I do wonder what you wanted to have happen when you called my parents place in early summer. I also wonder why you didn't return my call at the end of July when I, returning from four months in Winnipeg, eventually got the message about your call. Little mysteries that nag.

And I also hope you don't mind me having sent this letter to you - somehow when I have good thoughts about things you seem to be included and wanting to share things with you is, to me, always a good thought too. I don't want to ever forget you, Jason, and addressing a letter to you once or twice in a blue moon is the least I can do to keep your memory alive.

And someday, Jason, I'll flag you down for another coffee. I'll get another chance to see who you are and who you are becoming.

Ian

Ian Moar
**** Riverview Circle
COCHRANE
932-****

January 15th, 1999

Jason;

I'm in Cochrane for a month or two as my dad is dying of cancer and I'm here to help both my parents cope with that situation. And even though I harbor reservations about contacting you (probably because I'm just setting myself up for another rejection) – I mustn't just let the opportunity slip by.

The easiest way for me to remember you, Jason, is just to read the two or three letters you wrote to me a couple of years back, and when I do that it rejuvenates and clarifies for me again what a unique and valuable character you are. I would sure love to know how the intervening years have increased or otherwise affected that value. I would like to discover more of who you are now.

Jason - I'm presuming you're attending university and are buried under with all the things you do - but if you have any interest in having coffee together, could you just give me a call or write me a line? I guess if no contact is made then the damage we did to each other way back then is still insurmountable and I'll have to finally adjust myself to that reality. I just hope that isn't true - that both of us can muster the courage to continue a relationship well worth continuing.

But remember too, Jason, that if it's still too difficult to handle, I'll always appreciate who you are and who you've been in my life. But I'd also like to hear about all the things you've learned and all the things you've seen since I saw you last. I'd like to pay attention to you again.

Ian

Ian, January 27, 1999

To say that I was surprised to hear from you would certainly be an understatement. I've been staring at the letter that you sent me for almost two weeks now, as I have been unsure as to how to proceed. I must admit that a great deal of thought and feeling have gone through my mind lately, as I too remember what we shared and how much we inspired each other. However, I am also reminded of the way in which we both responded when we encountered a misunderstanding and I believe that maybe it has taken us these last two years to learn from our mistakes. I don't want to give you the impression that I regret what I did, because I don't....I only regret the manner in which I did it. I feel that although we have a great deal in common, we also have many differences and I think that perhaps it is those differences that are keeping us apart right now.

The question then becomes; what do we do about these apparent differences and are they enough to keep me from meeting with you for coffee? Well, my honest response to that is yes, for now. I need a little more time to think about what has transpired between us but I wanted to contact you and let you know that I do appreciate the letter - but now is not an acceptable time to get in touch. My reality is very different than it was back then, and although I am still the same person inside, my life has changed. It is difficult to describe in detail what has happened in my life, but nevertheless I harbor reservations about creating a new reality with you again. I guess we'll just have to wait and see what happens. I will write you or call you when I feel that I can open my life up to you and me again.

Jason

PS: I am sorry to hear about your dad.

February 5th, 1999

Jason;

I'm sitting at a writing desk in a beautifully-furnished lounge at Agape Hospice in Calgary. Dad's been here for a week and will unlikely last another. He's heavily medicated and in a deep sleep right now and I thought I'd use this chance to write to you.

At the outset I want you to know that I never intended to write after I received your letter earlier this week. As usual, you tidied things up and clearly defined the situation and nothing further from my end was required.

However, as the days passed by and after thoughts regarding you continued to float through my mind, I discovered that I do want to write, that I do have things to add - and that my contributions are worthwhile.

I thought it purposeful to just let you know where I'm coming from these days, Jason - at least in relationship to you. You tell me that your own particular situation or reality is far different than when I knew you, and perhaps you need to know how parts of my reality have also changed and how others have stayed the same.

Risking redundancy, my highest appreciation of you, Jason, always surrounds my perception of how you see things, how you understand things, how you express things, how you reverberate to the situations you find yourself in. I think the world has failed to produce 'ideal' characters like it has the potential to produce and you have always struck me as being 'closer' to that 'ideal' in some aspects than others I have known.

I have always admired how you handled us. Remember that we have neither role models nor modeling to help us out, Jason - so every way we act or react is exactly the best that we can do at that instance, and as you state in your recent letter, no apologies are required.

I suppose the biggest lesson I personally learned from our previous relationship, Jason - was that I needed to give up the idea of ever finding someone to work with, someone with a similar vision who could stand by my side. I have quite a battle ahead of me and however strange it seems, I guess I have to fight that battle utterly alone. You were thorough enough, we went far enough in our relationship, to scrape those longings for partnership from my soul.

I think before I imagined that I could somehow relate to you 'face-to-face,' Jason - where we could connect directly and powerfully and to then discover what doing that could bring. Even then I knew that our differences were as significant and as valuable as our similarities. You had a crispness and a clarity of vision, a directness, that I appreciated. You had a way of accurately defining goals which encouraged their manifestation. You were on your road to somewhere and, by God, I knew you were going to get there.

Now the proper way for me to regard our relationship, I think, is to see it as being periodically 'side-by-side' - where I acknowledge that you are exactly who you are and are going exactly where you plan to go. I see myself as just someone who would occasionally like to walk up beside you and ask you how things are going, to ask you what you see and why you think you see things that way. It's your perspective, those actual differences, that add value to my own voyage. I see none of it as threatening, but rather the very stuff the best things inside my own being are made from.

My sense on reading your letter, Jason, is that you're apprehensive about resuming things where we left off. I think I told you that the amount of energy I put into whatever happened previously was intense and that it had to be in that particular set-up. I suspect that if we met for coffee you would find me still capable of being energized by whatever transpires, but pretty placid in being able to stir up any of your old anxieties. Maybe the difference is that I know what I need from you, Jason, as opposed to what I might once have wanted. Those 'wants' were undoubtedly attachments of various types to you - now I just need whatever comfort the experiences and insights of another conscious being can bring into my life.

All I'd like to do is just sit and hear your stories, Jason. I can learn things and I can teach things in an environment like that. I really enjoy allowing my energy to be pointed your way, as in this letter, and equally enjoy it when I feel your energy touch my life.

What I don't know is whether or not you need someone or someone else to pay that type of attention to you, Jason? I suspect that when you say your reality has changed, that it now includes others. That instead of just saying 'I' you might just as easily now say 'we' from whatever vantage point you're at. And I must admit I'm intrigued by the mystery of your new reality. I wonder how it answers and satisfies the questions and longings you always had? I wonder if you've been able to maintain your integrity and consistency of values and goals in whatever comfort zone you've discovered?

And that old imagination of mine kicked into gear at wondering exactly what situation was home for you now? And why would it be difficult for you to describe it? Were you married now with maybe a child to take care of? Had you found religion and become a member of some cult or re-born Christian group? Perhaps you had a medical disease or suffered some serious accident that altered your physical reality big time? Or maybe it was a question of sexuality? My mind didn't wonder much further than those four. Each one would certainly put you in a different place than when I knew you. Most would also be difficult to describe adequately in short manner.

But I sure as hell hope you don't believe I'd do heavy numbers on you about whatever it is, Jason. I think I'm pretty good at both understanding and respecting the pathways each of us as individuals take to get through life and any you take, young man, would only line up metaphysically with everything else that you've done and will inevitable do.

You once spoke from a very solitary position. You have spent a great part of your life being unique but being very alone. It sounds like whatever changes have come into your life have altered that aloneness and I can imagine some gratefulness on your part for that. Whether it's real, lasting or substantially valuable are things you'll only learn in time.

Just try to erase from your mind, Jason - that we would just pick up where we left off. As you yourself said, your whole situation has changed enough to make you see things differently than before. And my expectations have changed. Maybe whatever business we had with each other is over. Maybe we derived everything from our relationship that was there to derive, although I sense there is a great deal of value in each of us that we can continue to share.

I recognize your tension and apprehension as you think about us reuniting. I am pretty casual about it all, Jason. I regard you as being a significant person in my life and I just want to see how you're doing and who you are. I think I'll always be legitimately intrigued by who you are and am therefore interested in what you're doing and why you're doing it. And you certainly have always been strong enough to have somebody pay attention. But maybe you simply don't need that anymore - maybe you're getting more than enough attention in whatever surroundings you're in. Maybe I'm barking up a tree that just doesn't exist anymore.

Anyways. . . . those are the things I've thought about this week when I've thought of you. Thank you for your letter, Jason - it sounded difficult to write and I wish I didn't bring so much unease into your life. But I do like the way you mull things over. I do like the way the most fundamental parts of each of our beings are affected by the life and the movements of the other. You're pretty sharp, kid - and I'm pretty sure I'll value and appreciate you all of my life.

And thanks for reading this.

Ian

Appendix;

Author's note; In the early to mid-90's I got quite embroiled in the politically-sensitive social issues of the time, both locally in British Columbia and in Albert, while I was there - like women's and minority rights. This is a typical contribution of mine, although certainly too long to have been considered by the local paper as a typical 'Letter to the Editor.'
Please note the date of the contribution and try to remember, if you can - the atmosphere regarding those issues at the time.

Ian Moar
Kelowna, B.C.

Letters to the Editor
The Kelowna Capital News
Kelowna, B.C.

March 6th, 1995

Dear Sir;

On reading any of Paul Robinson's recent diatribes regarding homosexuality, I can understand how his attacks would get labeled 'homophobic.' For a phobia is an 'irrational' fear, something beyond reason - and his homophobia, which is the Christian Fundamentalist one, should invite a far deeper inquiry into his bigotry than just assuming that it comes from the tired old Bible-based injunctions he so proudly preaches.

I sense the answer to his deep-seated hatred is also beyond the psychiatric assessment that hating homosexuality seems to be a function of being afraid that you might be one yourself. That fear would be a 'rational' one, and we could expect dysfunctional behaviour from such a fear, considering the hateful social climate bigots like Mr. Robinson continue to promote. The one our silent majority sanctions.

Before I contribute my own insight into why Christians always go crazy about queers, may I respond to several of Mr. Robinson's opinions presented in his supposedly 'fact-based' letter printed March 3rd.

He states that his arguments can stand on medical and scientific evidence alone, and yet it is the scientific community itself that destroys his extremely biased position.

Mr. Robinson states; "As to differences in the brains of homosexuals, that is opinion, not science." Well, Mr. Robinson, why not let us determine if the following is science or just opinion?

1) At the recent annual meeting of the Society for Neuroscience in Miami Beach, Florida, ground-breaking research was presented by psychiatrist Sandra Witelson of McMaster University showing the region of the brain known as the corpus callosum, believed to govern higher learning functions, is 13% larger in gay men than in heterosexuals. This suggests there is a 'neurobiological component' in human sexual orientation.

2) In 1992, University of California (Los Angeles) School of Medicine scientists Laura Allen and Robert Gorski reported that a brain structure called the anterior commissure is 34% larger in homosexual males than in heterosexual males. This suggests a biological link to homosexuality.

3) Again in 1992, neurologist Simon Levay of the Salk Institute for Biological Studies in San Diego reported that the hypothalamus - the part of the brain that regulates appetite, body temperature and sexual behaviour was much smaller in gay men than in heterosexuals.

All three medical and scientific studies suggest that these changes or differences in the brain occur before any particular behaviour develops and probably takes place before birth. And these three studies, Mr. Robinson, certainly outweigh your simple-minded, non-scientific and extremely ignorant 'opinion' that sexual orientation is a 'conscious' choice, which can easily be changed. If you have an imagination, Mr. Robinson, try determining how easy it would be for you to try to become a homosexual.

You also say in your letter that you harbour no animosity towards the many homosexuals you have known in your life, but you are disgusted by what they do and with whom they do it. Let's put our cards on the table here. If 'what they do' means anal intercourse, then you should know that researchers surveying heterosexual men who practice both anal and vaginal intercourse with their wives or girlfriends or with prostitutes, a full 60% prefer anal. That tells me the practice and enjoyment of anal intercourse is therefore not a function of being gay, but of being male.

When you say you are disgusted with whom homosexuals do it with, then you're taking a mighty swipe at who people love, not just who they make love to - and even your God isn't allowed that freedom.

Which, in a round-about way, gets me back to wondering about your homophobia, Mr. Robinson. There seems to be something very basic, something at the soul-level, about one man loving another man that really scares most males - certainly right-wing religious ones. Because your 'irrational' attitudes and hateful behaviour can't logically be attributed to anything you've revealed to us in your letters. It's gotta come from someplace else.

Maybe what's really behind your homophobia is this - that you yourself are terrified of being loved by a man - that you somehow subconsciously sense that it might actually comfort you - that you would respond positively to it, and perhaps even discover that it actually uncovers a profound and more mystical depth of love than heterosexual love affords.

Secondly, the only judgment that ever really exists for we as humans is whether or not we have loved our fellow man, which would also reveal the love we have for ourselves. Subconsciously you know that you'd fail that judgment and your subsequent frustration and anger manifests itself in hatred towards other men you sense are trying to achieve that, rather than in the healthier desire on your part to change and grow.

Therefore, your homophobia displays your irresponsibility in loving and being loved by your fellow man. You fail, in the end, to be able to truly give or receive. You reveal your unwillingness and inability to even love yourself, and the rest of us are simply left with your disgustful hatred of gays.

In one way I wish, if you had some decent shame, that you'd just crawl back under the rock you came from instead of flaunting your ignorance and hatred before us. On the other hand, people like you actually become lighthouses for the rest of us, warning us away from the shoals of hatred that has become your foundation. Seeing you and what you do helps us from being shipwrecked on the same shores, and I need to be thankful for that - so you do serve a worthwhile function.

And since you've been granted the space in this paper to offend decent human beings and especially homosexuals, let me now be offensive to you. Did you know that Biblical scholars, not secular ones, have surmised that your St. Paul was most likely a repressed homosexual? And that his inability or unwillingness to maturely deal with that issue twisted his behaviour towards others and this would help explain both the misogynist and anti-homosexual attitudes that have pervaded Christian thought for two thousand years.

And I would suggest that if your own Jesus walked the earth today He himself would be considered gay. His whole character, his sensitivity, his advanced level of consciousness and different way of seeing things, would line up far more closely with homosexual rather than heterosexual characteristics. Also, Jewish males in his day and age were considered 'different' or 'musical' or any other term you'd care to insert, if they were beyond twenty-two years of age and still unmarried.

You know, there's been a lot of argument about 'gay rights' lately. Personally, I believe religious freedom should have a far lower legal protective status than it does. Your religion just tells us what you happen to believe. It's not what you are. If people need protection from hatred and abuse, then what we are becomes far more important than simply what we believe.

Intelligence, imagination and education can't alter one's racial origin, one's gender or one's sexual orientation - but they can certainly alter one's beliefs. So if I had to choose between protecting the legal rights of a homosexual trying to survive or the rights of religious zealots like Mr. Robinson, who just want to spew their hatred - then my choice, without hesitation or doubt, would go to the homosexual.

And I think if Mr. Robinson devoted half the energy of his anti-gay campaign into learning about objectivity and authentic spiritual growth, then he would quickly move beyond the tyranny of his present belief system.

Yours truly

Ian Moar